to Billable Hours

Boo to Billable Hours

---

a lawyer's guide to better billing

John Derrick

Podia Press
Santa Barbara, California

First published in 2008

ISBN: 978-0-9797778-0-6

Library of Congress Control Number: 2007932548

To order this book, visit www.amazon.com

Podia Press
Santa Barbara, California, USA

Table of contents

PART FOUR: BETTER BILLING

WRAPPING UP

Introduction

Mention the term "billable hour" in the context of the practice of law and you'll typically be met with reactions ranging from a wince to a jaded, perhaps even conspiratorial, smile.

What you probably won't encounter is anything very positive. Although the billable hour dominates the way in which legal services are charged, remarkably few people speak about it with any enthusiasm.

Across large parts of the legal profession — as well as among clients and law students — the billable hour is widely criticized, often loathed, and even ridiculed. During the past 10 years, moreover, some of the sharpest criticisms have been heard from within the heart of the legal establishment. With this has come growing interest in alternative forms of billing.

Despite that, few predict the billable hour's demise. The legal profession is, for the most part, reluctant to mess with the golden cow that feeds it.

Why read this book?

So given that criticism of the billable hour is already widespread, and given that the system is unlikely to go away, what's the point of reading this book (or, for that matter, of writing it)?

Part of the answer is that the book critiques the billable hour from a different angle. The criticism that is commonly heard is that lawyers have come under pressure to bill *too many* hours. Often, the concern is expressed from the point of view of what this does to the quality of lawyers' lives, rather than from the perspective of what it means to the client. That is a legitimate concern, but it doesn't address the inherent flaws of charging for legal services by the hour.

Excessive hours make the problem worse. But the problem goes much deeper than lawyers not being home in time to put the kids to bed.

As I'll show, the issues of excessive billing targets and inherent flaws are separate but interrelated (and I'll be examining both). What I'm trying to do is to challenge the assumption that — even with reasonable annual targets — the billable hour is rational or desirable as the dominant form of billing.

So what's the problem?

The billable hour is touted as a clean system in which clients pay for what they get in a transparent and linear manner. In practice, however, the process of recording billable time involves a host of arbitrary, irrational, and suspect practices. Far from transparently reporting time expended, it distorts it.

This isn't just a matter of deliberate bill padding (although that is the "elephant in the dining room" whose presence in the profession many would prefer to overlook). Rather, the problem results from the nature of the time-recording protocols that are inherent to the process — for example, the assumption in just about all lawyers' hourly billing systems that the lowest increment of recordable time known to humankind is six minutes and the belief among many lawyers that it is actually 12 minutes.

Then there are the arbitrary decisions about when the meter is turned on and off. Not to mention the ethical issues involved in selling the same time twice. And so forth.

Only by looking at the minutiae of how time is actually recorded in different situations in which lawyers find themselves can one fully understand the billable hour's intrinsic flaws.

But the problems with the billable hour extend to more than its inherent distorting effect. The whole system rewards the plodding, inefficient lawyer and penalizes the skilled lawyer who completes a task quickly and effectively. Furthermore, it takes no account of *value* delivered, nor of the nature of the task performed. In addition, it chills the attorney-client relationship.

Making a difference?

Will this book make any difference? The answer is that nothing — let alone one lawyer's book — is likely to prompt a mass exodus from hourly billing.

But change can come one lawyer at a time. Those with small-firm or solo law practices are especially able to redefine the way they charge for their services. Law students have choices as to how they want to spend their careers, and they can begin to look for those corners of the profession where the billable hour does not reign supreme. Clients have choices, too.

I *know* that alternative billing can work. I have a law practice that eschews the billable hour. In my practice, I generally offer flat-rate billing. But there are other alternatives, too, and this book walks you through a number of them.

Bit by bit, alternative billing can make advances, not to the extent of toppling the mighty billable hour, but by chipping away at it and establishing that there *are* other ways. My hope is that this book will encourage readers — be they lawyers, clients, or law students — to think about some different choices.

The alternatives

This book is subtitled *A Lawyer's Guide to Better Billing*. And, as indicated, the book is not just about criticism, but also about examining alternatives and applying a critical eye to them, too.

That said, the bulk of the book is taken up by an attack on the billable hour – the book's main title suggests as much. This isn't negativity for negativity's sake. The reason is that the need for alternatives rests largely on the flaws of the status quo. It's not that the alternatives are flawless. It's more that the billable hour is worse. "Better billing" requires an understanding of that premise.

Ultimately, my conclusion is that no form of billing is perfect – although some are less flawed than others. It may be that some form of hybrid is the best solution in many cases.

Some might argue that this book is "biased," because of the opinions it expresses. Actually, it isn't. I make no apologies for expressing opinions, but I came to this subject with an open mind.

Nonetheless, I expect to receive some flak for the views I express. That's fine. It goes with the territory of speaking out against the norm. Actually, it's encouraging – if a book like this doesn't get under some people's skins, it isn't doing its job.

A note to law students

For the most part, law schools don't do much to educate students about billing practices in the legal profession. The first exposure that many students get is if they are hired by a law firm as a summer associate. But this is when the law firms are on a charm offensive. Summer associates will likely be spared the more brutal and demoralizing aspects of the billable-hour regime.

That said, summer associates will probably be told something like: "Record all your time." With that imperative, law students enter the world of private practice. But those four words do little to explain the numerous practical and ethical issues that recording time actually involves.

If you read this book, you'll learn more about the billable hour in practice than you likely will from any law school class or law firm recruiter. It might well put you off the billable hour. But you might decide to enter the world of the billable hour nonetheless — even if you agree with much of the criticism expressed.

And the reason is that a lot of cutting-edge and interesting law is practiced in environments where that type of billing is the norm. Even if you don't want to spend your entire career recording your actions in six-minute increments, you may decide to experience that world before making other decisions later on.

So I wouldn't necessarily advise against working in environments where the billable hour dominates. Just go in with your eyes open. Use this book as a guide. And set your own standards.

If you do decide — now or later — that you *don't* want to work in a billable-hour environment, there are opportunities in private practice to escape it. But one of the best sanctuaries is, of course, government service. Along with the retirement benefits, freedom from the billable hour counts as one of the great perks of public-sector law practice.

An important proviso for clients

This book is written primarily for lawyers and future lawyers. However, it's also good reading for clients of lawyers. The message is the same whoever you are — the book is not about trying to advocate a system of billing that makes sense for one constituency based on short-term interests but, rather, to invite everyone with an interest in the practice of law to think about what is rational, fair, and sustainable all around.

But there's one important proviso about this book that clients should keep in mind: It would be foolish to choose or reject [illegible] w firm solely because of the method of billing. This [illegible] about billable hours, so there's much discussion about that subject. But, ultimately, of greater importance than the method of billing is the quality of a lawyer's work. In some ways, the billing culture can impact quality of work, but there is far more to good lawyering than good billing.

There are many excellent lawyers who — although operating with what I consider to be an intrinsically flawed hourly billing method — do perform excellent work and, often, for reasonable prices. If you are a client, and you are happy with the service you receive and feel that the price is fair, you may not really care all that much about the method by which the bill was calculated.

Let me give a couple of examples from my own experience (although I should add that this book is not littered with my personal war stories).

Before I became a lawyer, I owned and ran a niche publishing company, which I eventually sold. I used the services of a lawyer who billed by the hour to represent me in the sale. He did an outstanding job. His bills were fair. Frankly, I wasn't bothered by *how* the bottom-line numbers on his invoices were reached.

I would much rather have paid him by the hour than to have gone to some below-average lawyer who happened to offer "alternative billing." (And, as a reminder, half of all lawyers are, by definition, below average. As are half of all dentists and car mechanics.)

Likewise, when I became a lawyer, and before I set up my own practice, I worked for a law firm that generally billed by the hour. I did good work for its clients. Other lawyers in the firm did so, too. Indeed, I continue to refer clients to them.

But not all clients have unbridled admiration for their lawyer. Often, clients stick with a lawyer as a devil they know, but question whether they are getting great value or brilliant service. And, often, their doubts are justified.

In cases such as that, the type of billing method can swing the difference between there being, overall, a satisfactory or unsatisfactory experience. Moreover, as I will show in this book, billing cultures and methods do impact quality of work when lawyers are stressed more by "making their hours" than by getting results for their clients.

The billing method may not be the be-all-and-end-all of the practice of law, but it is a key aspect. The more debate there is on the methods, the better.

Where is the counter to this book?

Which brings me to another point: *Where is the book that defends the billable hour?*

With all the criticism of the billable hour, there is remarkably little out there written in its defense. That is why I end this book with a challenge.

The structure of this book

The book you are holding is divided into four parts. Part One provides a short introduction to hourly billing and shows how we got to where we are today — it turns out that the billable hour only established its grip on the legal profession in the second half of the twentieth century.

Part Two dissects the billable hour, pointing out its flaws — both those that are intrinsic and those that have arisen or have been exacerbated as a result of the increasing numbers of hours that lawyers are expected to bill.

Part Three shows how there has lately been a backlash and asks why the billable hour continues to be so strong despite criticism and a general lack of enthusiasm. It also discusses the rules governing the practice of law that impact billing.

Part Four examines the alternatives. This includes a list of better ways to bill by the hour for those who cannot wean themselves off the clock, as well as analysis of completely different methods that shift the focus away from time and onto value.

Finally, the book wraps up with a short conclusion.

Enjoy the book. If you're a lawyer, battle on while enjoying the practice of law — one way of doing so is to think differently when it comes to billing. If you are a law student, take it from me that it is a great profession and you can find corners where you can get away from aspects that you find off-putting. If you are a client, choose your lawyer with care.

If you want to recommend this book to others, tell them to buy it at Amazon.

I made a few minor revisions to this book in 2009. I won't be updating it further. There has recently been a fair amount of coverage in national media about law firm billing. But I have said what I wanted to say. Time will tell how much, and how quickly, things will change.

John Derrick
Santa Barbara, California

Part One: Background

1. Billable hour basics

Most lawyers charge for their services according to the amount of time they spend delivering them. The idea is that a lawyer records time spent on a matter, usually in increments of one or two tenths of an hour. At the end of the month, bills are prepared that multiply the number of hours logged by the lawyer's hourly rate.

"Seems simple and logical," you might be thinking. "So what's the problem?"

Read on and you'll find out. But first, some further introduction.

Hourly rates

Less experienced lawyers generally have lower hourly rates than the more seasoned, to take account of the fact that they supposedly perform less sophisticated work or take longer to perform the same tasks. (That said, some who are not so seasoned charge high hourly rates in order to appear more experienced.)

Hourly rates vary considerably, with big-city and big-firm rates generally being higher than others. Across the board, rates are generally between $150–$600 per hour depending on location, firm size, and experience, but they can be lower or higher.

"Blended rates"

Sometimes, law firms offer something called "blended hourly rates." This means that the firm offers a client a fixed hourly rate regardless of which lawyer is doing the work (and, as with regular hourly rates, regardless of the nature of the work being performed). Not many firms offer that as a matter of course, but some clients with clout demand it and get it.

I don't have particularly strong views on the "blended rate" concept. Arguably, it makes budgeting a little easier, because the client doesn't have to factor in the variable about which lawyers in a firm will end up doing what work. But it doesn't seem to address any of the fundamental problems with the billable hour that will be discussed in this book. And it can give a law firm an economic incentive to assign its least experienced attorneys to a particular task — so it's not that clear why clients would want it anyway.

Log-'n'-bill

As lawyers perform their work, they keep a log describing the tasks as well as recording the time spent. In the olden days, this was done on paper "timeslips." Today, it's done using timekeeping and billing software.

At the end of each month, bills are automatically assembled from the time entries that were entered over the course of the month. If more than one lawyer worked on a matter, all of the different lawyers' time entries are consolidated on a single bill.

Typically, one of the lawyers — probably a partner or someone else in a supervisory role — will then review the bill before it's sent out. This provides an opportunity to edit or remove certain time entries.

However, the reviewing lawyer is not necessarily looking out for ways of reducing bills. Moreover, that lawyer may have had little — and perhaps no — involvement in the case during that month and so may not possess a good, first-hand sense of exactly what work was done or needed to be done.

Thus, unless time entries seem obviously in need of downward adjustment, they will generally be left as they are. In that case, the bill that goes out is not the product of some assessment of value. Rather, it is simply a mathematical function of the time entries.

So if there were 24.3 hours recorded by lawyers charging $275 per hour, a bill will issue for 24.3 x 275 = $6,682.50. "Kaching" goes the cash register.

But, as this book will show, the recording of those 24.3 hours turns out to be a more arbitrary and questionable procedure than the apparent precision of the number might suggest. I'm not just talking about "bill padding" (although that can be part of the problem). Rather, there are problems inherent in the process of measuring a lawyer's time.

The four types of time

When I first became a lawyer and joined a firm, I was presented with a simple directive: "Record all your time." But the more time I spent lawyering, the more I realized that a lot of "time" should not even be recorded, let alone put on bills. Time spent looking for lost files, time spent managing my time, time spent distracted, and so forth.

Even though information about this time might aid a law firm administrator's efficiency analysis, there's a good chance that, in practice, once recorded, it would find its way onto a bill — especially if euphemisms were used to refer to what was taking place (e.g., "investigate status of matter" instead of "look for mislaid file").

So not all time is — or should be — "billable." And, later in this book, I'll be discussing what a realistic ratio is of total to billable time.

So far, therefore, we have got "time spent" and "billable time." However, time can also be categorized in two other ways.

The term "billable hour" does not necessarily refer to the time for which a client actually gets charged. Rather, it refers to time that a lawyer logs in a timekeeping system. But — as pointed out above — some of this time may be written off, such that it never finds its way onto a bill. To put it another way, there is a difference between "billable hours" and "billed hours."

In some environments, there is little difference between what is "billable" and what is "billed." Just about all time that gets onto the time logs ends up on a bill. In others — and especially where those in charge are sensitive to the issue of "value" — the spread can be greater.

Then there is a fourth measure of a lawyer's hours. As well as "spent," "billable," and "billed" hours, there is also the measure of what is "collected" (i.e., paid by the client).

Ideally, what is collected will match what is billed. In reality, that isn't always the case. Sometimes, clients challenge bills and lawyers then issue credits. On other occasions, clients simply don't pay — and lawyers write off balances.

Generally, when people in the legal profession talk about "billable hour targets," they refer to the goals for billable time that is recorded — not to goals for billed or collected time (although separate targets may exist for these). Thus, if a law firm expects junior lawyers to bill for, say, 2,000 hours, it doesn't necessarily expect that they will generate 2,000 times their hourly rates in actual revenue.

However, the larger the gap between the number of hours recorded and the numbers billed and/or collected, the more of a question mark may hang over the quality of a lawyer's work.

That might be unfair. A lawyer with a very low billable-to-billed spread might simply be benefiting from a general policy of writing off very little, whereas a high spread might be indicative of a more value-driven billing approach.

Even within the same law firm, some partners may be more prone to writing off time than others. (Decisions about writing off time can become very political, incidentally. Partners or senior associates can draw bitter resentment when they write off their subordinates' time and not their own.)

Theoretical transparency

To some, the attraction of hourly billing is that, theoretically, it removes the more subjective aspects of certain alternatives. The client essentially buys a lawyer's time, during which that lawyer devotes best efforts to advancing the client's interests.

Because lawyers are obliged to account for time, they keep records that show not only the duration, but also the nature, of the work performed. There is — in theory, at least — transparency and accountability.

The reality, however, is somewhat different. But I'll get to that later. First, some history.

2. How we got to where we are today

The billable hour began to dominate the legal profession in the last few decades of the twentieth century. However, its roots extend back almost 100 years. Ironically, in view of the connotations of greed that surround it today, its inventor was someone more often remembered as the father of legal aid in America.

Mr. Smith starts the clock

Early in the twentieth century, a lawyer named Reginald Heber Smith took over the running of the Boston Legal Aid Society, a provider of legal services to the indigent. And, in 1919, he authored a seminal book titled *Justice and the Poor*. This was a study criticizing unequal justice based on wealth.

As United States Supreme Court Justice Ruth Bader Ginsburg said in a lecture in 2001: "Smith exposed vast differences in the quality of justice available to the rich and the poor. His exposé led to endeavors to narrow the gap, including the establishment of the first national legal aid organization.... [He] galvanized a national movement to provide lawyers for those who could not afford to pay counsel."[1]

But as Justice Ginsburg added: "[Smith] did not neglect the remunerative side of work in the law. Among his other distinctions, [he] is credited with inaugurating the practice of calculating lawyers' fees by billable hours."

---

[1] Lecture entitled *"In Pursuit of the Public Good: Lawyers who Care."* Delivered at the University of the District of Columbia, David A. Clarke School of Law, April 9, 2001.

The clock started in 1914, when Smith — who had graduated from Harvard Law School — asked the Harvard Business School to help him devise a system to track and manage the Boston Legal Aid Society's finances.

Out of this arose the then-novel procedure that staff lawyers should begin keeping detailed records of their time spent on different cases. This was not for billing purposes — the Society's services were provided free. Rather, it was a management tool to help ensure that resources were deployed effectively.

Later, Smith went into private practice and took with him the accounting system he had devised in his legal aid work. He became an evangelist for the recording of time, and influential in the subject of law practice management. Hence, daily time sheets found their way onto lawyers' desks next to the blotters, pens, books, and other tools of the trade.

"The statement that a law office needs an accurate cost accounting system seems revolutionary," Smith wrote in 1940, "but if every business concern has to know its costs, why should the law office be immune?"[2] To him, the hour was the commodity: "The service the lawyer renders is his professional knowledge and skill, but the commodity he sells is time."

Blazing the trail for billions of time entries that were to follow, he added: "We use the hour and the tenth of an hour because it facilitates not only addition but other calculations.... For convenience in figuring nothing surpasses the decimal system."

---

[2] Quotations from Reginald Heber Smith in this paragraph and the two that follow were included in an article on law.com dated November 25, 2005 — *The Billable Hour: Are Its Days Numbered?* — by Douglas McCollam of *American Lawyer* magazine. The article did not cite the source. However, Smith wrote a book called *Law Office Organization*, which went through numerous editions published by the American Bar Association, all long out of print. The quoted remarks may well have come from one of those.

Looking back many years later, Smith — who died in 1966 — wrote that while he thought "nothing could be simpler" than a form on which you recorded the client, the name of the matter, and the time you spent working on it, the lawyers at his firm hated the practice. Indeed, Smith wrote, it "seemed to them little better than a slave system."

Early timekeeping

Although formal timekeeping became routine in many law offices during the 1940s and 1950s, the practice of calculating bills simply by multiplying time by an hourly rate did not catch on immediately.

Rather, for most of the 20th century, lawyers sent out bills that attempted to assign value to the services that had been rendered. The amount of time spent in performing the services was always an important factor in setting the amounts. And, inspired by Smith and his disciples, law firms began tracking time in a more organized manner.

But timekeeping was, initially, more of an internal reporting procedure than something that directly controlled billing. Moreover, time tended to be recorded in something of an impressionistic manner.

The rise of the billable hour

Today, the bean-counters of the legal profession love hourly billing, whereas clients are often wary of it. At the outset, however, the roles were reversed.

Early pressure for time-based billing came from the client side of the relationship. This is because clients began to resent the mystery that lay behind the assignment of dollar amounts on lawyers' bills at the end of descriptions of services rendered.

Many began demanding answers to the question: *"Well, how long did this actually take?"*

In order to appear responsive, law firms began producing their time records to clients. Thus, information that previously had been maintained solely for internal management purposes was put on center stage in the billing process. Law firm consultants then discovered that by making bills a simple mathematical derivative of time, there was an opportunity to raise revenues.

As a result, by the start of the 1970s, most mid-sized and large firms had shifted to billing solely by the hour for the vast majority of their work. Small firms and solo practitioners for the most part followed along.

Hold-outs to the billable hour

The big exception to hourly billing was the "contingent fee" — the "no-win, no-fee" gamble that is common on the plaintiff side of the bar in personal injury, wrongful death, employment, and professional malpractice litigation.

However, for the most part, the contingent fee targets a very different segment of the legal services market from that tapped by the billable hour. It is generally used as a means of providing legal services for plaintiffs who would not otherwise be able to afford a particular type of lawsuit and where there is a reasonably good chance of significant monetary recovery. As shown later in this book, when one talks about "alternatives" to the billable hour, contingent fee billing (at least in its pure form) is not what one generally has in mind.

Another notable hold-out has been the criminal defense bar. Although a fair number of criminal defense lawyers do bill by the hour, flat-rate billing is far more common in their line of work than in civil litigation. I'll be talking about this later in the book when I discuss the viability of flat-rate billing in litigation generally.

That said, these hold-outs should not obscure the billable hour's ascendancy. They are the exceptions, not the rule.

How the U.S. Supreme Court boosted the billable hour

A United States Supreme Court decision in 1975 helped cement the billable hour's position further. Until then, county bar associations in many parts of the country laid down minimum fee schedules for certain types of legal work. The idea was that it was "unlawyerly" to compete on price and that minimum prices had to be maintained in order to uphold professional standards.

Although these rates were — at least, for the most part — set as "minimums," they became, in effect, the flat fees that all lawyers observed in the areas covered. And lawyers who didn't observe the fee schedules risked disciplinary action by their state bar.

The Virginia State Bar, for example, warned that "evidence that an attorney habitually charges less than the suggested minimum fee schedule adopted by his local bar Association, raises a presumption that such lawyer is guilty of misconduct." The American Bar Association's model ethical code that was in effect until 1969 proclaimed that it was unethical for an attorney to "undervalue" legal services.

As much as I am a supporter of flat fees (as will become clear later in this book), I am not a believer in cartels. And officially mandated prices are about as bad a system of setting fees as I could possibly imagine.

Fortunately — although surprisingly late — the Supreme Court held in 1975 that the setting of minimum fees for legal services amounted to a form of price-fixing that was illegal under the Sherman Act.[3] Freed of the controls under which they had previously labored, many lawyers who had not yet switched over to hourly billing took the opportunity to do so.

It seemed at the time to be the modern alternative and the wave of the future. Back then, flat rates — which, today, are spoken of as a progressive alternative — seemed tainted. The free market beckoned with the billable hour.

Early doubts about the billable hour

It was not long, however, before some in the profession began to question whether hourly billing was good for the practice of law. In the late 1980s, the American Bar Association set up a task force to look into the prevalence of hourly billing and to examine alternatives.

This resulted in a study published in 1989 called *Beyond The Billable Hour*. The ABA study began by noting that "[c]lient dissatisfaction exists with respect to hourly billing." The task force's Chairman, Richard C. Reed, wrote in the foreword: "Perceptive lawyers have long realized that hourly billing often rewards the inefficient practitioner and penalizes the well-organized efficient lawyer."

One of the study's contributors was Mary Ann Altman, a lawyer who founded Altman Weil, a prominent consulting firm providing services to the legal profession. She wrote that she was "involved personally in the introduction of time records to the legal profession" 30 years earlier. However, she candidly admitted to the problems of billing by the hour, including the fact that "very few lawyers keep truly accurate time records."

---

[3] *Goldfarb v. Virginia State Bar*, 421 U.S. 773 (1975).

Billable hour inflation

In the last 10 years of the twentieth century, the billable hour came under further scrutiny. The cause was not simply concern that hourly billing was not a rational or efficient way of charging for legal services, but — rather — that it was having a bad effect on the way that law is practiced.

Lawyers were being motivated by the numbers of hours they could bill. Many, indeed, were becoming obsessed by maximizing hours in order to enhance their reputations among colleagues and bosses. Others were burning out, such that the profession was losing good people. Fewer were finding time for pro bono work.

These criticisms were fueled by sharp increases in the numbers of hours that law firms expected those on their payroll to bill, a consequence of salary wars that took place as top firms vied with one another to recruit the brightest and the best.

Concerns about the billable hour carried into the new millennium, with some very high-profile voices — including at least one member of the U.S. Supreme Court — beginning to speak out on the subject. In 2002, the American Bar Association published a further critical study.

I'll be returning to this later, and quoting examples of the types of criticisms currently being voiced. I'll show that the basis for much of the contemporary criticism is not that the concept of billing by the hour is, per se, misguided, but that the legal profession has begun to impose excessive expectations on itself as to *how many* hours lawyers should bill.

I agree that the billable hour has gotten out of control in that regard. But some of the emphasis on excessive numbers of billable hours misses the point that the concept is flawed at a more fundamental level.

How to critique the billable hour

So before talking about the billable hours explosion of recent years, I want to show why relying on timekeeping as a complete means of charging for legal services is intrinsically prone to create anomalous, arbitrary, and other undesirable results.

To do this, it is necessary to look at the detail of how lawyers actually account for their time — and the decisions they need to make every day in completing the electronic time records that are the successors to the time sheets invented by Reginald Heber Smith.

Only by looking at the detail can one understand the true nature of the problem. That's what's missing from the "big picture" analyses that focus only on the total numbers of billable hours, as opposed to the protocols by which those hours are measured.

In the end — as I will show — the two strands of the problem converge and feed on one another. However, they should still be examined separately in order to understand each of them.

Part Two: What's Wrong?

3. Built-in obfuscation

At the end of the last chapter, I explained that in order to understand what is wrong with the billable hour, it isn't sufficient just to join in the mantra that lawyers are under pressure to bill too much time. It's also necessary to look into the minutiae of what is actually involved in keeping time records. Only then does one see the inherent flaws of a billing policy that relies more or less entirely on those records. So, down to detail...

Daily totals

The billable hour promises transparency. In practice, what clients often experience is obfuscation. This occurs with even the most basic aspects of the billable hour's implementation.

In most firms, lawyers keep daily records of how much time was spent on matters, but do not separately record the time spent on individual tasks during a day that relate to each matter.

Assume, for example, that a law firm represents a client with several different "matters" that are active — a "matter" might be a lawsuit, a transaction, an area of ongoing advice, or whatever. Time for that client is typically recorded and billed separately for each matter.

Usually, however, time is not broken down by "task" within each matter on those days when more than one task was performed. Thus, a typical daily time record might read:

> Telephone conference with opposing counsel re objections to discovery requests. Letter to opposing counsel confirming points agreed. Start to research

> and write motion for summary judgment. Telephone conference with client on developments. Travel to and interview with Fred Smith, witness, at his office. 4.8 hours.

In that example, the client receives a figure for the total amount of time spent on a given day, but not the time that was devoted to each different task.

Did the conference with opposing counsel take three minutes or 10 or 20 times that amount? Is one paying for 15 minutes of travel time or two hours? Was the legal work on the motion a major chunk of the day's work, or just a quarter of an hour?

This clearly reduces the transparency that hourly billing is meant to provide.

Monthly totals

In fact, some lawyers who bill by the hour only provide monthly, not daily, totals. These make it even harder to figure out how much time was spent on which tasks.

Under that protocol, an invoice sent out by a lawyer who charges by the hour contains a consolidated description of work performed over a month. That description ends with a time total for that month and, perhaps, a list of the dates on which any work was performed — but *without* an indication of what work was performed on each of those dates, let alone how long it took.

That method appears to offer the worst of all worlds. It doesn't address the fundamental flaws of hourly billing that are discussed in this book. But it deprives the client of much of the information that supposedly makes hourly billing worthwhile.

To be fair, proponents of this method may also suggest that the overall descriptions of the month's work should be detailed. They simply don't want lawyers to tell clients too much about *when* work was done and *how long* each portion of the month's work actually took. Rather, the client is expected to trust in the lawyer to present an accurate bill, which doesn't invite scrutiny with regard to those details. It's a system dictated by the interests of the lawyer, not the client.

Monthly descriptions make sense if the method of billing is to assess value rather than simply to multiply hours by an hourly rate. Indeed, that was how bills were typically presented in the era that predated the onslaught of the billable hour. But if one is going to charge by the hour, monthly totals deprive the client of information that ought to be disclosed.

Recording time for each task

At the other end of the scale from lawyers who report only monthly totals are those who record time for *each task* during the course of a day (as opposed to keeping a cumulative total for all tasks related to a matter on a given day). In fact, some insurance companies who fund the cost of defending lawsuits demand this.

A lawyer operating under such a regime would have reported the time entry given earlier something like this:

> Telephone conference with opposing counsel re objections to discovery requests: 0.1 hours
> Letter to opposing counsel confirming points agreed: 0.2 hours
> Start to research and write motion for summary judgment: 1.0 hour
> Telephone conference with client on developments: 0.3 hours

Travel to interview with Fred Smith, witness, at his office: 2.7 hours
Interview with Fred Smith: 0.5 hours
TOTAL: 4.8 hours

On the whole, lawyers don't like keeping time records by each task. It is, in fact, quite time-consuming in itself. (That raises the issue of whether the client should pay for the time that it takes to manage the timekeeping. Many clients do end up doing so, although few would be very happy if they knew about that.)

And it exposes lawyers to greater scrutiny. It's harder to fudge details if all the time entries for a given day are broken out than when they are merged together.

At first glance, therefore, task-based timekeeping seems better for the client, as — in theory — it's the most transparent and accountable approach. However, as shown in the following chapter, it can backfire on clients who demand it, as it forces lawyers to apportion at least six minutes to individual tasks that might not have taken nearly that long.

If you think that six-minute charges are too small to be worth worrying out, think again. Three of them a day can easily add up to over $2,000 a month. (If you're wondering how, a six-minute charge based on a $350 hourly rate equals $35; three of those a day equals $105; multiply that by the number of working days in the month and you get past $2,000.)

This doesn't mean that, after weighing the pros and cons, I necessarily favor day totals over task-based records. In my opinion, the billable hour is flawed *whichever* way you try to implement it.

4. The anomaly of the six-minute minimum

No matter whether time is recorded on a daily basis or a task basis, a one-minute phone call that is the only task on a given day will always be charged at a minimum of six times the time it actually took. (Unless the lawyer chooses not to bill for the call at all, but don't count on that.)

And the reason is that six minutes is the lowest increment of time that can be recorded using the systems under which almost all timekeeping lawyers operate.

Likewise, a seven-minute phone call that is the only billable event on a given day will cost twice as much as a single six-minute one — $60 versus $30, if the hourly rate is $300. In other words, the extra minute over the first six will be charged as a further six minutes.

This does not quite square with the notion that hourly billing is all about charging clients for what they receive in a simple, linear manner. Far from being transparent, the system of recording time in one-tenth increments of an hour actually has an inherent distorting effect — one that results in clients paying for more time than they actually receive.

One could, in theory, devise a timekeeping system that allows increments of as little as a minute. However, I am aware of none that is out there. In practice, the decimal system devised by Reginald Heber Smith — see Chapter 2 — reigns supreme.

Six-minute minimums and task-based reporting

The anomaly of the six-minute minimum is magnified when time is recorded by the task, rather than the day. If a lawyer makes 10 separate two-minute telephone calls, each of which has to be recorded and timed individually, the lowest amount of time that *can* be recorded is 60 minutes. This is because each call would be charged at 0.1 hours (i.e., six minutes), even though it only took a third of that amount of actual time.

Thus, clients who demand that time be broken down to the maximum extent might not be doing themselves any favors. Unless lawyers choose not to bill for some calls, they have no option other than to bill 10 times for 0.1 hours in that example.

I suppose that a lawyer could batch the separate calls as a "single task" — but that really gets away from the premise of task-based timekeeping. The lawyer who labors under that type of timekeeping regime doesn't have much incentive to depart from it on an ad hoc basis simply in order to keep the bill down.

Lawyers who work with daily totals, by contrast, could put down 0.3 hours for the 10 calls combined — corresponding to the actual time, 20 minutes, that they took.

However, some lawyers who do report daily totals would *still* end up charging 0.1 hours per call, resulting in the charge of one hour. In other words, even if they are not required to *report* times for each task, they might still choose the task-based *counting* method if it makes for a higher total for the day.

This is especially likely to occur if the calls are made over the course of a day, with other tasks occurring in between. And it is all the more likely to occur when there is a general "pressure-to-bill" culture in the law firm.

Is all this talk about minutes petty?

Some readers may be wondering whether it is all a bit petty to fixate about extra minutes being charged here or there. And, at some level, going on about this does lower the tone of the practice of law. But those minutes add up. Lawyers who rack up 2,200 hours of billable time a year do not get there by being loose with their minutes — they try to grab every one that is available.

It is the legal profession, not clients, that has started this. By choosing to make a system of counting minutes central to the practice of law, the profession invites scrutiny about how those minutes are actually recorded. It would be unreasonable to chide clients and commentators for pettiness in questioning lawyers' counting protocols, when it is the lawyers themselves who began the process of obsessing about minutes.

The British "unit" alternative

In Britain, timekeeping lawyers have come up with a way of dealing with the awkwardness of the six-minute minimum. Rather than bill time in "minutes," as such, they bill it in "units."

However, this amounts to exactly the same thing. That's because under the British system, one "unit" is equivalent to six minutes. So, although the two-minute call would be billed for "one unit," not expressly for "one tenth of an hour," it is, in effect, still a charge for six minutes of the lawyer's time.

From the lawyer's point of view, presenting the bill in "units" means that one is not expressly levying a six-minute charge for a two-minute call. It seems better from a presentation perspective — even though, substantively, it is the same.

But I'm not sure I would advocate going over to the "units" system. It seems nothing more than a method of papering over the billing cracks.

5. The highly questionable 12-minute rule

The distortion caused by billing increments becomes even worse when lawyers use 12-minutes as the minimum and incremental units of time.

Excuses for the 12-minute minimum

The 12-minute — or 0.2-hour — minimum is surprisingly common. Under that scenario, a lawyer making a three-minute phone call will bill for 0.2 hours (i.e., 12 minutes) — even though the timekeeping and billing software allows for increments of half that amount.

The usual justification for the 12-minute minimum is something like this: "Time is lost ramping up for, and ramping down from, each task. The three-minute phone call actually takes more than three minutes out of my day. It disrupts my flow on the work I was doing immediately before and afterward. This needs to be compensated."

A flaw in this reasoning is that it assumes that the three-minute call does interrupt some other flow. But the call could be preceded by a task that was already complete — another phone call for example. It is fanciful to suggest that all short calls somehow disrupt some other activity.

Also, there is already compensation when, say, a three-minute call is billed as 0.1 hours — i.e., the difference between three and six minutes. One doesn't need to go all the way up to 0.2 hours even if one were to accept the "ramping up" and "ramping down" premise.

Furthermore, one hopes that the timekeeper who insists on 12-minute minimums will be as avid at stopping the clock on a task that is interrupted as at starting it on the three-minute call that disrupts the flow. Otherwise, the lawyer would be selling the same time twice. Consider the following example...

A lawyer starts work on a document for Client A at 2:00 PM and finishes at 3:00 PM. So the lawyer bills Client A for an hour. Sounds fair.

But in the middle, the lawyer took a three-minute call relating to Client B — not a huge interruption, but still enough to bill Client B for 0.1 hours or, maybe, 0.2 under the 12-minute rule. But that may *not* be enough for the lawyer to reduce the one-hour charge to Client A — after all, it was "only" a three-minute interruption.

So this lawyer has defied nature in extracting more than sixty minutes from the hour. The practice of law can seem like a time machine.

The indefensible 12-minute increment

The 12-minute minimum is bad enough. Worse, still, is when not only does time start at 12 minutes, but it also goes up in 12-minute increments. For example, a phone conversation would be billed for no less than 0.2 hours — corresponding to 12 minutes — and, if it ran longer, it would jump to 0.4 hours.

What about 0.3? The whole "ramping up" and "ramping down" argument is inapplicable here — you can't logically charge for two ramp-ups and ramp-downs with a single conversation. Despite this, some lawyers do, indeed, operate on the basis that time progresses in 12-minute amounts after the first 12 minutes. But others who use 12-minute minimums draw the line at 12-minute increments.

The ethics of 12-minute billing

A word here about ethics. I'll start with an analogy. I actually do not think that most politicians in this country are corrupt. The number who would take a briefcase full of hundred dollar bills in return for a favor is really quite small.

That said, we live under a system that is, at some level, institutionally corrupt. Money is needed to run politics. Money does not grow on trees. Nor is it funded by the state. So money is donated.

And those who donate the largest amounts are those who hope to buy influence. If they gave the money in briefcases to individual congressmen, it would be criminally corrupt. But we have come up with an elaborate system, which — despite various gray areas — allows money to be given to politicians legally.

Now back to the practice of law. I do not think most lawyers are dishonest or cheats. Some may be, but — in my experience — lawyers are not, collectively, a bad breed of people. However, some operate under a set of rules that, at some level, is institutionally dishonest. This includes rules that make the smallest measurable unit of time 12 minutes.

Fortunately, I don't think that 12-minute billing is the official practice in most law firms. Corporate clients tend to be savvy buyers of legal services and would rebel if they saw this in fee agreements. But I suspect it is more common at an individual lawyer level. By that, I'm not pointing the finger at solo practitioners, in particular, but also at individual lawyers in firms of all sizes.

Faced with pressure to bill high numbers of hours (a topic I'll be turning to later), the hungry lawyer needs all the minutes that are out there. The temptation to go up by 12-minute increments proves too much for some to resist.

And the knowledge that it is not all that uncommon allows minute-hungry lawyers to persuade themselves that they are not being individually dishonest but merely conforming to a professional "custom and practice."

6. The problem of accuracy

Minimum increments are not the only anomaly arising out of hourly billing. Another is that billing is not as exact a science in practice as it is meant to be in theory.

A reality check about time records

Even with the best of intentions, it is very hard for lawyers to maintain time records that are completely accurate. If one is multitasking, and being interrupted by phone calls and other distractions, it requires a discipline that not all possess in order to keep records that one knows to be totally accurate (even putting aside the built-in imprecision of the six-minute minimum and the like).

Indeed, as noted in Chapter 2, one of the contributors to the American Bar Association's first study on billable hours — a leading law practice management guru — opined that "very few lawyers keep truly accurate time records."

The more the timekeeping is done in "real time" (i.e., with time recorded as soon as a task is complete), the higher the accuracy. However, in practice, real-time records, while aspired to, are not always kept.

All too often, therefore, lawyers come up with their best estimates of time at the end of a morning or day during which they juggled several balls. Some even try to reconstruct their time at the end of the week or month.

This might work to the client's advantage. Ethical lawyers tend to under-record time when they are unsure of the total. Often, tasks are forgotten.

Then again, it might work to the client's disadvantage — especially in environments where lawyers are under pressure to bill high numbers of hours.

But whether the inherent problems of accurate timekeeping work to the client's advantage or not, the important thing to realize is that timekeeping is very often a more makeshift process than its proponents generally care to admit. And if time records cannot be counted on for accuracy, why, exactly, does the profession rely on them so heavily?

7. The price-value disconnect

Thus far, I have talked mostly about practical anomalies and difficulties arising out of hourly billing. But there are more fundamental objections to the billable hour — ones that focus on the disconnect between the amount that is charged and the value that is delivered.

The more you know, the less you get

Let's assume that Client A comes to me with a legal problem and we agree that I will bill for my time spent dealing with it. The problem Client A presents is within my general area of competence, but it involves some legal research and analysis. I spend three hours and bill accordingly. All typical stuff that occurs in law offices every day.

A month later, Client B comes to me with a quite similar problem, which I also agree to handle on an hourly billing basis. Because of the time that I spent on the earlier matter, I can handle Client B's problem in only one hour and I bill accordingly — i.e., for one third of the amount billed to Client A.

One can debate whether Client A paid too high a price, or whether Client B got a bargain. But what is clear is that one of them paid three times as much as the other for the same overall value.

Of course, lawyers who feel they are learning on the job often do discount their bills for time spent figuring out how to do what the client may have assumed they understood already. But this does not necessarily occur. It's especially unlikely to occur if the lawyer reviewing bills containing other timekeepers' entries doesn't really know how much "learning" occurred. And the client probably doesn't have a clue as to how much "learning on the job" took place.

Moreover, it can be hard to distinguish between a situation where the lawyer is learning on the job, in such a way that a client shouldn't be picking up the full tab, and one where research is simply an inherent part of the task. Unless one handles only the most cookie-cutter matters, the practice of law is all about finding things out. In that sense, there is a "learning" element in just about every matter — especially litigation, which, if done properly, generally involves extensive legal research.

And if the correct approach to hourly billing is to discount time when it includes too much of a learning process, then why not have a system that formalizes some form of value-oriented billing? Why only correct for overcharging on a piecemeal, unsystematic basis, where there is a good chance that adjustments will be applied inconsistently, if at all?

High bucks for mundane matters

Another aspect of the price-value disconnect is that a fair amount of the time spent by lawyers involves doing unskilled, undemanding things for which one barely needs a law license:

- Driving to a deposition.
- Sitting in court waiting for a hearing on a motion when there are 10 cases in front of yours.
- Taking part in a conference call in which one's role is very limited.
- And so on.

Usually, those sorts of things are charged at the same hourly rate as legal work that is highly skilled. But why should they be?

The stock answer given by defenders of the system is that by sitting there performing the undemanding task, the lawyer loses the opportunity to do sophisticated legal work at that particular moment. This answer relies on the premise that lawyers who aren't sitting in traffic or waiting in court *would* be doing sophisticated work at that very moment.

But there is no inherent reason why that premise should apply. They might at that very moment be doing some other *unskilled* task. Or they might be doing nothing at all.

The argument about charging the full rate for unskilled time works only if there is an assumption that lawyers have enough highly skilled, hourly paying work to fill every hour they are willing to work — such that doing any unskilled work for less money would lead to a loss of revenue. That may hold true for some — but it is probably not true for most.

The arbitrariness of unitary hourly rates

What the analysis above shows is that lawyers who apply the same hourly rate across the board are disconnecting price from value in two respects: First by charging the same for their time regardless of their experience level in a given skilled task; and second by charging the same regardless of whether the time is spent doing something that even requires skill. By having a unitary hourly rate regardless of the skill possessed or required, they charge what amounts to an arbitrary amount.

If one is going to charge by the hour, a more rational and less arbitrary approach would be to set, say, three hourly rates for each lawyer. The one that would be applied would vary depending on how skilled the lawyer was in a particular task and how much skill the task required.

No doubt this would itself lead to anomalies, gray areas,

and arguments. But it seems less arbitrary than applying a unitary rate to cover all the work a lawyer does.

The under-appreciated brilliant hour

The price-value disconnect rewards some lawyers, but leaves others under-compensated. By charging simply for time spent, the lawyer misses out when inspired and skillful work is performed, which delivers considerable value but happens not to take very much time.

The billable hour delivers an irrational set of incentives. The fact that service is performed quickly should be grounds for *extra* reward. In practice, the lawyer who delivers quickly is penalized. The one who profits under the billable hour is the plodder who struggles or meanders to complete a task or resolve an issue. The point was made eloquently in an article in the *Harvard Law Review* back in the days when the billable hour was still a relatively new concept:

> "One thousand plodding hours may be far less productive than one imaginative, brilliant hour. A surgeon who skillfully performs appendectomy in seven minutes is entitled to no smaller fee than one who takes an hour; many a patient would think he is entitled to more."[4]

The lethargic hour

At the other end of the scale from the brilliant hour is the one in which the lawyer devotes 60 minutes to the client's affairs, but is simply not very productive or inspired.

---

[4] George D. Hornstein, *Legal Therapeutics: The Salvage Factor in Counsel Fee Awards*, 69 Harvard Law Review 658, 660 (1956).

I would say that most of us are on our peak form at certain times of the day, and off our peak at others. The human body rarely delivers consistent performance at all times. Mine certainly does not. There are times when one is either slow or when, lacking drive, one resorts to tasks that can best be described as "near-work experiences" — activity that at some level is related to the mission, but that barely counts as work. (Fixating on the choice of exhibit tabs. Re-reading one's work product, but more to admire it than to improve it. Or whatever.)

There is nothing to be ashamed about if you experience these tendencies. Lawyers are not automatons. But the billable hour takes no account of these natural fluctuations in human energy and work intensity. The meter ticks away at a steady pace, oblivious of the amount of drive that is present and adrenalin that is pumped. Every hour costs the same, regardless of whether it is an optimum exemplar or one that is sub-par.

Unfair to cabbies?

Above, and at various points in this book, I refer to the "meter" ticking away. The implication, perhaps, is that lawyers charge in much the same way as cabbies — the most visible operators of ticking meters.

But this might be unfair to cabbies. With most taxi meters, the tab is calculated using a paradigm that combines time and distance. If you're stuck in a traffic jam, the meter will go up. But it will go up more quickly if you're making rapid progress to your destination.

So the taxi billing model is value-related. The taxi driver's meter makes more sense than a lawyer's. If my references to "meters" suggests that I am accusing taxi drivers of charging like lawyers, then I apologize to the cabbie profession.

8. The incentive to overlawyer

Not only is efficient lawyering undercompensated through hourly billing, but overlawyering is encouraged.

The issue is somewhat analogous to cost-plus contracts, where a contractor marks up every sub-contractor's and supplier's bill and thus profits the more the client is charged.

Just as the cost-plus contractor has no financial incentive to keep the price down once hired for the job, so the lawyer who charges by the hour has little incentive — at least in the short term — to keep down the hours billed. To the contrary, the lawyer's incentive is to bill as much as possible. The result can be unnecessary lawyering.

Of course, it isn't always easy to draw a line between what is and is not "necessary." In many areas of the practice of law, it is very hard to determine when a task is "finished" — absent a deadline that forces it to come to a conclusion.

In litigation, for example, it is rare that a document is beyond the point where it could be improved if only more time were spent on it. Even the most gifted writer's output can usually be improved by further editing. Indeed, it is the gifted writer who usually *demands* more editing. Likewise, one can lose all sense of time while conducting legal research and often be uncertain when enough is enough.

Nonetheless, the fact that there is more that *could* be done does not always mean that more *should* be done. There can be a diminishing return. And there is such a thing as "busy work" in the practice of law — activity that fills up time sheets but does not really lead anywhere productive.

Moreover, there are often ways in which one can get to where one needs to go simply by being efficient. However, the whole problem is that the lawyer who is laboring under an employer's expectation of high billable hours has no incentive to try to reach desired ends in as fast a manner as possible. The lawyer needs to rack up those hours. And the hours, more often than not, will go straight onto the bill.

The impact of technology on the billable hour

The tension between efficiency and the billable hour is all the greater because technology has enabled today's lawyer to perform some tasks far more quickly than was the case only two or three decades ago.

Legal research is a great example. In the days of hard-copy legal research, finding authority and then checking to see whether it is still good authority — "Shepardizing," to use the verb derived from the provider of the original tools for this purpose — was a hugely time-consuming exercise.

Today — using online tools such as Westlaw and Lexis — one can often achieve in minutes what, previously, would have taken hours. And one can do so from one's desktop, without shuffling around a law library.

However, operating on a time-based billing system, the lawyer loses out in this situation. An old-timer who insists on researching the law the old-fashioned way might charge for three hours to come up with an answer to a question. However, the lawyer who utilizes legal technology to its fullest can do the same in, say, 30 minutes.

On a time-based model, the old-timer would get paid six times as much to reach the same conclusion. That makes no sense.

There's another aspect to the efficiency gains made by the use of technology in the practice of law. If technology enables lawyers to complete certain tasks in, say, one sixth of the time that it used to take, does this mean that they get to go home early? Maybe, if they are their own boss. But, if they work for a firm, they still have to meet their billable hour targets.

This provides lawyers with a disincentive to perform a task as quickly as technology might allow. The problem with completing a task is that one immediately has to find a new one to perform in order to stay on the billable hour curve.

The quarter-of-a-million-dollar motion

It is not just the individual lawyer who has an incentive to rack up hours even if this risks overlawyering. The problem extends, at a collective level, to the firm itself. The whole system is based on billing as many hours as possible. So firms typically do not train their lawyers how to be frugal in the delivery of services. They have no more reason to do so than a shoestore owner has in instructing salespersons to suggest to customers ways of making their old shoes last longer.

At the time of writing this book, I had just litigated an appeal involving, in part, an award of attorney fees. A large law firm in Los Angeles charged about a quarter of a million dollars for preparing a single 20-page motion — with some supporting declarations — involving no discovery. This reflected about 600 hours of billable time. The firm claimed that this constituted the "reasonable" attorney fees that it was, supposedly, entitled to recover from my clients — the opposing parties — under a California statute with a "loser-pays" fees provision. The trial court awarded these fees and my clients appealed.

Putting aside the question of whether there was an entitlement to fees in the first place, I cannot accept that spending 600 hours on a single motion with no discovery *can* be reasonable. It reflects a billing culture that is out of control, involving work by lawyers who have no incentive to keep the time spent proportionate to the nature of the task.

I won that appeal for my clients. However, the appellate court did not reach the issue of whether the amount of the fees award was unreasonable, as it reversed on other grounds.

One benefit of smaller law firms is that, typically, they don't have the resources to bill such excessive numbers of hours in the first place. Likewise, lawyers who are very busy — and who don't have legions of underlings to whom work can be delegated — tend to be forced to be efficient simply in order to manage their workload.

So by no means do all lawyers meander through their days trying desperately to fill up timesheets. The circumstance where this does occur tends to be in environments with too many lawyers operating under too high expectations about how many hours they are meant to record.

9. Billing for thinking

The under-appreciated brilliant hour — discussed earlier — is not the only example of how hourly billing can operate to a good lawyer's detriment. Another is the fact that time spent thinking can often fall between the cracks and go uncompensated.

Action versus reflection

It is rare that the verb "think" appears on lawyers' bills when they account for their time. That is not to say that most lawyers do not think as they act, but there is often a sense that "thought" on its own isn't something that clients want to pay for. There is a tendency, therefore, to stress words that connote action rather than reflection.

Thus, it is rare that a lawyer who bills by the hour comes up with a billing entry that read something like:

> "Thinking. 0.3 hours."

Rather, time entries tend to detail actions, as opposed to contemplation. For example:

> "Letter to..."
> "Draft document..."
> "Review document..."
> "Appear at..."
> "Prepare for..."

Of course, time spent thinking can be dressed up in terms

that connote action. For example: "Prepare for oral argument," rather than "think about what to say at oral argument." (One lawyer who read a draft of this book told me that he uses "analyze" as his preferred term for thinking — but that word may not be sufficiently action-oriented for some.)

But why do lawyers so often feel obliged to engage in that type of window dressing? Thinking is a huge part of a lawyer's job. Who wants a lawyer who doesn't think hard about a client's case?

The answer probably comes down, at least in part, to billable hours. Clients are suspicious of the ticking meter. The notion that it is ticking away when a lawyer is not actually "doing" anything makes people feel uncomfortable. There isn't enough accountability.

How much "thinking" should start a meter? How does one separate out "thinking" that advances the client's case and "thinking" in the sense that one is simply reflecting on the task at hand (e.g., worrying about the amount of work or planning one's day, as opposed to, say, mentally drafting a legal argument).

Where exactly — and under what circumstances — was the "thinking" taking place? And was the time spent thinking recorded immediately, or is the lawyer relying on a recollection of the thought process?

Time in the shower and riding your bike

Personally, I quite often find myself thinking hard about a client's case in the shower or while taking a bike ride or in other contexts far removed from a traditional law office setting.

I don't generally bill by the hour, so the issue of whether to charge for this time does not arise with me. But what if I did? I suspect that clients would have a problem paying for shower time. But if I didn't charge for this, I would be "giving time away" — which is what the hourly timekeeper isn't meant to do.

Obfuscation about thought

Of course, the lawyer can get around the "shower time" issue by simply not reporting *where* the thought takes place. But there is still the problem about simply reporting "thinking" as the activity, regardless of the location. Hence, the thought process in the shower — if it is to be compensated at all — will end up being billed vaguely as "preparation" for whatever activity is at hand or will be merged into some overall description of a day's activity.

That way, the lawyer gets paid. But the payment relies on obfuscation. And, for billing purposes, obfuscation is the opposite of transparency. So, once again, the "transparency" argument that is trotted out to support hourly billing is found to be at odds with what actually occurs in practice.

And something is surely wrong when "thought" — which is at the core of a lawyer's work — is something that a practitioner is embarrassed to admit to.

Multiple meters

One of the most thorny issues concerning "billing for thinking" occurs when lawyers in the same firm spend time caucusing in collective thought. Clients do not always understand the value of brainstorming and frequently complain when billing entries appear from multiple timekeepers indicating that they were "conferencing" with one another.

Their skepticism is enhanced if the conferencing lawyers record different amounts of time. The fact that lawyers can report different lengths for the same event speaks to the imprecise nature of time recording generally. It does not inspire confidence. Inconsistent time entries ought to be corrected when bills are reviewed prior to being sent out, but sometimes aren't. Of course, discrepancies will be hidden if the conferencing time is part of a batched daily total that also includes other tasks. That daily total can cover up a multitude of things.

In any event, sensing client resistance to paying for lawyers in a firm to talk to one another, attorneys often try to find creative ways of dressing up their descriptions of the powwows in which they engage. Anything to avoid use of the tell-tale word "conference." Again, so much for transparency.

The price of brainstorming

There may be much value in brainstorming, but it is also very expensive. It's bad enough with two lawyers' meters ticking away, but a third or fourth can really result in shocking bills — the thoughts that come out had better be good for the amount that can be charged. Yet the value-per-lawyer tends to go down the more that are involved, with some participants having only marginal input.

On the other hand, not to brainstorm seems wrong in itself. If the ticking meter chills creative thinking, the billing system is getting in the way of the job.

So I don't know what the ideal solution is. I am not an advocate for hourly billing, and I certainly don't have a solution to all its difficulties — other than simply discounting the bill when a 30-minute conference seems ridiculously expensive in retrospect. My preference would be not to bill by the hour so that these issues don't have to be addressed.

Time spent delegating

Keep in mind that "together time" between lawyers isn't always focused so much on brainstorming as on giving direction. This can be also useful — for example, 20 minutes spent by a senior attorney in conference with a junior colleague can give focus to the latter's effort and avoid hours of wheel spinning.

Arguably, however, the delegation of a task from one lawyer to another is an internal, administrative function relating to a firm's resource management for which the client should not be charged — or, at least, for which only one lawyer's time should be charged. It isn't the same as brainstorming where multiple lawyers all add value. However, as throughout this analysis, there can be gray areas.

Wrapping up thought

Wrapping up my thoughts in this chapter about thought, I am of the opinion that lawyers *should* be compensated for productive thinking — whatever the billing method chosen. That applies whether the thinking is done alone or by brainstorming with colleagues. (That said, some thoughts are, of course, more worthy of compensation than others.)

My concerns are that with hourly billing, thought becomes a line item on a bill — rather than simply being part of the essence of the service — and that the lawyer has to deal with gray areas about which thoughts are billable and often then feels a need to disguise the process of thinking as something else.

In addition, it is much harder to record the duration of thought in an objective manner than it is to record time devoted to actions. Thought can be fleeting. It comes and it goes. A client has to have considerable trust in a lawyer to accept uncritically a line item on a bill devoted to thought alone.

Moreover — as I indicated at the start of the chapter — the whole thought issue often works against the hourly-billing lawyer, as, in practice, thinking time frequently does not get recorded. (Although some might say that this is the system's way of compensating for ways in which other time gets bloated.)

So the concerns about arbitrariness, vagueness, and obfuscation that run throughout my analysis of the billable hour are present here. There are better ways of being compensated for thinking than running a meter.

10. Double billing

In the last chapter, I talked about multiple meters when lawyers caucus. However, by "double billing" — the title of this chapter — I refer to something different. I'm not talking about two lawyers both billing for time spent together. Rather, I'm talking about *one* lawyer trying to extract 120 minutes out of a single hour when two clients are involved. The question is whether this can be justified.

One task for two clients

A classic example is when a lawyer has two clients with aligned interests in the same matter, each of whom is billed separately. Nothing wrong with that (assuming that all the rules about conflict letters and waivers that apply in the particular jurisdiction have been observed).

But assume, for example, that the lawyer has a one-hour telephone call with opposing counsel discussing matters that implicate both of the clients' interests. Does the lawyer then bill each of the clients for an hour? Or is the bill split, so that each client only pays for 30 minutes?

Personally, I think the ethical answer should be obvious. Lawyers who bill by the hour — on the basis that time is the commodity they are selling — cannot have their cake and eat it.

If clients were billed by *value* — as opposed to by the hour — then the value given to one client would not be diminished by the fact that similar value was being given to another. Value is not a finite commodity, which has to be sliced up. Unless a fee agreement provides otherwise, there is no inherent reason why

Client A should pay less just because Client B is also benefiting — or vice versa.

Time, by contrast, *is* finite. It cannot make intellectual or ethical sense for a lawyer billing by the hour to charge the same hour to more than one client — even in a scenario where both clients benefit from that hour. The bill should be split.

Double billing the same time for different tasks (1)

Above, I talked about a scenario where two clients were billed for the same task in a given matter. Another variation of double billing involves billing the same time on unrelated tasks.

Assume, for example, that a lawyer goes to court for hearings on two unrelated matters in front of the same judge, both on the same calendar. The lawyer leaves the office at 8:00 AM for an 8:30 AM calendar. Client A's matter is called at 8:50 AM and concludes at 9:00 AM. Client B's is called at 9:15 AM and concludes at 9:20 AM. The lawyer is back in the office at 9:50 AM.

How does the lawyer charge the two clients? One would hope not by charging both for the entire time from leaving the office to returning. A 50-50 split would seem fair (although, arguably, Client B benefits more than Client A in the above example, because its full bill would have been higher).

Double billing the same time for different tasks (2)

Here's another example. Picture a lawyer on a flight from JFK to LAX on a business trip on behalf of Client A. And let's assume the lawyer is in Business or First Class (meaning that work is reasonably feasible in terms of the physical and mental space).

Let's put aside the issue of how travel time should be charged in general (I'll be getting to that in the next chapter). The issue to focus on now is this: What if — after swilling a glass of Chardonnay and deciding that the movie isn't worth watching — the lawyer pulls out a notebook computer and works on a document for Client B?

Let's assume that the lawyer was already charging Client A for the trip. Realistically, if Client A was willing to pay not only for travel expenses but also for travel time, it did not necessarily expect the lawyer to work on its behalf throughout the entire flight. That's not what people do on long flights. Client A probably wouldn't have minded if the lawyer had watched the movie.

But would Client A be happy about having the lawyer work for Client B on its dime? And is it fair to Client B if the lawyer bills it for work done during time that Client A has already paid for?

Under systems where lawyers bill for value and not simply for time, these questions wouldn't arise. No one would have bought the lawyer's "time," only the lawyer's services. And the client has no interest in *where* or exactly *when* those services are performed, so long as they are done within the required deadline and to the expected standard.

But it is the legal profession that has, collectively, rallied around and profited from the concept of selling time as its commodity — and so it has to deal with the practical and ethical issues that arise under scenarios such as the one just described. It can't just ignore these issues and fall back on a "value to the client" argument when it suits it.

Of course, in reality, Client A would never know that its lawyer worked for Client B on that flight. Likewise, Client B, when it received the bill, would never know that the work was done on a flight — let alone on a flight taking up time for which Client A was already paying.

So it comes back to the honor system. And the problem is

that in an age when lawyers are under huge pressure to rack up those hours — something I'll be coming to shortly — the need to do the "right thing" is in tension with the burning incentive to record time.

Lawyers who admit to double billing

Thus, the lawyer on that airplane could choose to double bill for the time and very likely get away with it. Likewise, the lawyer going to court for two hearings. And there is some evidence that this is exactly what a lot of lawyers choose to do.

In 2007, William G. Ross, a professor at Samford University's Cumberland School of Law, published a survey of billing practices in which he polled 5,000 attorneys from various walks of life throughout the country and obtained 251 responses.

Professor Ross reported that the percentage of attorneys who admitted that they had double billed was 34.7%, compared with 23% when he conducted a similar survey about a decade earlier. Moreover, only 51.8% regarded the practice as unethical in 2007, as compared with 64.7% in the earlier survey.[5]

The lawyers who do double bill in this manner might rationalize it internally by telling themselves that nobody is really worse off. Client A was happy to pay for that time, anyway. Client B was happy to pay for that work, anyway. So where is the harm?

Well, the harm is that the lawyer is, at some level, getting away with something. And that, ultimately, isn't good for the practice of law, in general — or for the attorney-client relationship, in particular.

---

[5] Professor Ross has also written a book titled, *The Honest Hour: The Ethics of Time-Based Billing by Attorneys* (1996, Carolina Academic Press). His Web site, which includes details of the attorney-billing surveys referenced above, is at www.williamgeorgeross.com.

11. The quandary of travel time

Travel time raises another question, besides the ones about double-billing: When should the clock start and stop?

Running the meter while traveling

Picture the following scenario: A lawyer flies from Los Angeles to San Francisco for a deposition beginning early in the following morning. (Anyone familiar with air traffic delays at San Francisco will agree that it would make sense to fly there the night before.) At 6:00 PM, the lawyer leaves the office and takes a cab to LAX. After the flight and a cab at the other end, the lawyer checks into a hotel at 9:30 PM.

At 10:00 PM, the lawyer has a late dinner in a nearby sushi bar, while reading a magazine. The lawyer then calls home, looks at the news on the television, and, after that, gets a good night's sleep.

Assume that this lawyer bills by the hour. The question is how much can be billed on that trip and on that day?

At a minimum, if the client is paying by the hour, the lawyer should be entitled to charge for the period from 6:00 PM to 9:30 PM — the journey time from the office to the hotel room. (The travel time should — in my opinion — be billed at a lower rate, as traveling is an unskilled task, but that's a different issue. Here we're talking about the *amount* of time that can be billed, not the *rate* at which travel time should be charged.)

But what about the rest of the time? Isn't it somewhat arbitrary for the lawyer to be racking up charges in one-tenth increments of an hour while shuffling along the hotel hallway, but then to abruptly switch off the meter simply on account of entering a hotel room? One does not have to be in motion in order to be traveling.

On the other hand, the meter surely has to be turned off at some point? The lawyer presumably doesn't expect to bill while sleeping. But exactly when does the meter go off?

This is a problem with hourly billing. Although it postures as an objectively scalable form of billing, with maximum transparency, it is actually rife with arbitrary judgment calls such as this.

And what about the sushi dinner? Probably, the lawyer will bill the cost of the meal, which is reasonable. But what about the time for the meal? Personally, I would not bill that time if I were laboring under an hourly billing regime. But others might.

Their reasoning would be that this is, in essence, part of traveling. And, in a way, they're right. If you charge for the time while you're eating a meal on a plane (assuming you are on one of the diminishing number of flights that serve them), why not then charge for your time when you eat a meal on the ground?

Presumably, though, you would have had dinner anyway? "Yes, but not dinner away from my loved ones or my other work," would be the reply. "This needs to be compensated."

One would imagine that even this lawyer would not charge for the time watching TV or calling home. But who knows?

Bathroom breaks while traveling? I won't go there.

Per-diem rates

Some lawyers who generally bill by the hour deal with travel time by applying a per-diem rate. In other words, if a client takes the lawyer away for a full day, it is still billed on a time-basis — but the unit of time is the day and not the hour.

This can make sense, but there is still the issue about what multiple of the hourly rate should constitute the day rate. A multiple of 12, maybe? Or how about 16 hours — i.e., 24 minus a notional eight for rest and recreation? But some trips might involve more than 16 hours of work in a day — a marathon mediation, for example. Essentially, this would mean the lawyer writing off the excess time. If the fee agreement provides for hourly billing, why should the lawyer do that on a trip, when there would be no such cap if the marathon took place without travel?

On the other hand, some trips involve long breaks between active lawyering. During those breaks, the lawyer might be catching up on other matters — which brings one back to the double-billing issue. So the problem is still that it's all pretty arbitrary.

That said, per-diem rates are, conceptually, headed somewhat in the direction of flat-rate billing — which, in my mind, is a *good* thing. However, a per-diem rate wouldn't work in the example given above about the San Francisco-bound lawyer whose travel on that day began at 6:00 PM. I suppose one could have a half-day rate as well. But even that could be excessive for a trip beginning in the evening.

A general absence of guidance and accountability

As I have acknowledged elsewhere in this book, all this agonizing about when to turn the meter on and off might sound petty and, to some, unprofessional. It is not the mighty cause that drove one to law school and to join this noble profession.

But the reality is that all the billing decisions analyzed above *are* going to have to be made under an hourly billing regime — whether one likes them or not. Typically, they will be made by the lawyer in private, with no consultation.

Very often, indeed, they will be made with no guidance

from the employing law firm (beyond the mantra that the lawyer should "record all time"). I've never heard of a law-firm manual that tells an associate when to stop and start the meter while traveling. (That said, I suspect that some firms might have these – and I'd be curious to see one should such a thing exist.)

So to argue that this is all too petty even to think about is, in essence, to say that the lawyer who needs to rack up hours should essentially be left alone to make judgments in private, without guidance and without the indignity of being held accountable.

That's all very well. But that type of blind trust in the system of hourly billing is one reason why the provision of legal services has become awfully expensive in recent decades. Those minutes and hours add up.

12. The chilling effect

Putting aside all of the problems of how to properly and honestly measure a lawyer's time, there is another concern about the billable hours system. If every time a client calls a billable-hour lawyer, there is the knowledge that the meter is ticking, a chill is placed on communications. This means that there is a disincentive to communicate.

On the whole, I think that is a bad thing. I say "on the whole," because there *can* be too much communication and there are some clients who, without disincentives, call their lawyer excessively. (Those are the clients a lawyer doesn't want anyway. I'll address that later when examining potential pitfalls of flat-rate billing.)

But, in general, a full and frank discussion of a matter results in a better attorney-client relationship and, often, in a better outcome. A lawyer is better apprised of the facts of the case and a client's needs. The client is better able to form realistic expectations. And it is a whole lot better to review alternative strategies before embarking on a path than to do so later as part of an inquest into what went wrong.

However, it is particularly galling for clients to find charges of $30 or $60 littered around their bills for very short conversations when they are already paying the lawyer a ton of money. Those sorts of charges are what make clients sense that they are being squeezed for every penny possible.

One way of addressing this is for the lawyer simply not to charge for short conversations with the client, even if the fee agreement calls for hourly billing in general. Quite a few lawyers do follow that commendable approach.

But, again, it comes down to the billing climate in which lawyers operate. If they are under pressure to meet targets, or laboring under a self-induced minutes obsession, they might feel that they can't afford to "give away" any time.

Moreover, the billing-obsessed lawyer may be especially reluctant to let those two-minute phone calls go unbilled. This is because, as noted earlier, those sorts of calls are the most "profitable" of all, since they're charged at a multiple of the actual length on account of the six- or 12-minute minimum.

13. Billing that puts a law license in peril

At what level does "aggressive" billing turn into dishonest — or even criminal — billing? That's a tough question. But with some regularity, lawyers are professionally disciplined and even criminally prosecuted for overbilling. Some go to prison.

Examples of lawyers who get into trouble

Generally, though, prosecution or professional discipline involves acts that go well beyond adopting questionable methods of accounting for time. To put your liberty or license in peril, you probably have to engage in some very deliberate, systematic fraud. Some examples:

- The former managing partner of a Manhattan law firm was sentenced to a prison term of 33 months for defrauding the Federal Deposit Insurance Corporation and the Resolution Trust Corporation of about $1.4 million by overbilling. The firm began submitting bills that substantially inflated the hours of work performed. The managing partner carried out his scheme by making handwritten notations on draft bills that directed the firm's office manager to increase the hours reported for individual attorneys, generally by one to four hours per day.

- A Milwaukee lawyer who billed the Office of the State Public Defender for 24 or more hours on each of 106 days pled guilty to a misdemeanor theft charge.

- A Florida attorney was disbarred for five years for overcharging a client by more than $2.5 million. The attorney turned in padded bills for an insurance investigation that he conducted on behalf of Lloyd's of London. He was found to have overbilled by $300,000 for his own work, by $1.2 million for the work of his associates, and by $1.2 million for expenses.

- A New York attorney performing work for a major Wall Street bank was accused of billing for hours not worked. He directed that actual time reported by associates be adjusted upward to meet desired billing levels. His secretary would first draft bills based on computer runs and then, at the lawyer's direction, would inflate attorney hours in order to hike the overall bills. That lawyer was sentenced to more than five years in prison.

- An attorney handling criminal appeals who bilked New York City's Assigned Counsel Plan with bills for thousands of hours of padded time was suspended for three years — a surprisingly lenient punishment. The attorney billed more than 7,600 hours for work supposedly performed on all but eight days of two years. (One of the extraordinary things about a story like this is that it took the administrators of the Assigned Counsel Plan so long to figure out that something was wrong if a lawyer was billing for 3,800 hours a year.)

- In perhaps the most famous billing scandal of all, Webster Hubbell — Hilary Clinton's former law partner who was appointed by then-governor Bill Clinton as Chief Justice of the Arkansas State Supreme Court and then went on to be the number-three person in the Department of Justice under Bill Clinton's presidency — was found guilty of over 400 instances of financial fraud, many of which involved overbilling clients. He was sentenced to nearly two years in prison.

Let me make one point clear, lest this book ruffles feathers more than is intended. The fact that I am talking about lawyers who engage in criminal conduct is not in any way intended to suggest that there is anything intrinsically dishonest about hourly billing.

Is hourly billing prone to being anomalous? Yes. Arbitrary? Yes. Irrational? Yes. Harmful to the attorney-client relationship? Yes. But intrinsically dishonest? No.

That said, a lawyer who pushes the envelope can stray from the merely arbitrary to the aggressive, and then from the aggressive to the unethical, and then from the unethical to the downright crooked. And it is quite difficult for clients and, indeed, colleagues, to know what is taking place. The billable hour involves a system that makes it easy for people to cheat and get away with it.

Most lawyers may do their best to remain honest within the system — even though that system has inherent distortions (such as operating on the fiction that the lowest amount of recordable time is six or 12 minutes). A minority exploit it for all that they can. Only a few of those get caught. At its best, it is an honor system. And not all who take part prove honorable.

Taking pennies out of the ethics jar

In the aftermath of an ethical collapse, one purpose of an ensuing autopsy is to discover where the problem began. Often, the answer is that there was no single act representing a massive ethical lapse that was the "but for" cause of all that followed. I suspect that most of the cases listed above did not begin with the lawyer suddenly deciding one morning to give up all the noble intentions that most people have when entering the profession and, instead, to become a criminal.

Rather, ethical spirals typically begin slowly when lawyers start taking pennies out of the "ethics jar" over prolonged periods — small ethical stretches here and there that, over time, lead to a distorted view of what is proper.

A constant series of close calls can end up creating a culture of amorality, if not outright immorality. Blind eyes are turned by others, perhaps. And then, in a small number of cases, things get really bad.

So there is nothing intrinsically "criminal" about taking the view that 12 minutes is the smallest amount of time that can be measured. Good people may have come to that conclusion. But, maybe, convincing oneself of the reasonableness of that obviously flawed proposition risks putting oneself on a slippery slope. Don't go there.

14. How common is bill padding?

The big question — which few in the legal profession really want to address, perhaps because they are scared of what they might discover — is how much outright bill padding does take place. There is some evidence that it may be more common than one would care to think.

Evidence of bill padding

In his already referenced survey, Professor Ross of Samford University's Cumberland School of Law asked lawyers whether they had "specific knowledge" of bill padding — i.e., invoicing a client for work never performed or exaggerating the amount of time spent on a matter.

Professor Ross reported that *two-thirds* of respondents said they had such specific knowledge. Respondents were not asked whether they themselves had taken part in such a practice.

Likewise, an article published in 2006 in *Law Practice Management,* a magazine of the American Bar Association, described what its author called "ordinary billing inflation or padding" — as opposed to the most "extreme" variety — as "probably rather common."[6] The same article referred to an unspecified 1991 study in which a majority of lawyers taking part estimated that five percent of all billed time was padding and one-sixth of those surveyed said 25 percent of all billed time was padded.

It's worth underscoring that this is not scare-mongering

---

[6] *Ethics and Time-Based Billing,* by Michael Downey, *Law Practice Management,* January 2006.

from the fringes of the legal profession. Nor is it mudslinging originating outside the profession. I am quoting from a recent article in a publication of the American Bar Association, no less.

The article — which originally appeared in the December 2005 edition of *St. Louis Lawyer* published by the Bar Association of Metropolitan St. Louis — went on to say: "Holiday distractions and year-end deadlines for bonuses and billable hours may make padding more common this time of year."

Degrees of padding

There is, indeed, a distinction between "ordinary" bill padding and the most egregious variety. It's not that the "ordinary" variety is okay, but the fact is that there are degrees. There is the systematic, truly shocking variety — especially carried out at a senior level in a firm — that results in the type of criminal prosecutions discussed in the last chapter.

And then there is the "ordinary" type where lawyers — under pressure to meet targets and anxious to keep their numbers on track — might, here and there, upgrade what should be, say, a 1.3-hour time entry into a 1.5-hour one. No single instance of padding may seem all that much, but, collectively, it adds up.

That said, it may often be a gray area as to how much, if any, actual "padding" takes place, because of the inherently imprecise nature of recording time in the first place (see earlier discussion about increments, arbitrary choices regarding when to turn the meter on and off, etc.).

The problem is that the profession seems, collectively, to consider its policing duty done when a few egregious padders are exposed and punished, while not really addressing the problem of lesser padding on a widespread basis. And, to be fair, padding is — as a practical matter — very difficult to police, short of having ethics monitors peering over shoulders with stopwatches.

That's one of the great pluses of flat-rate billing. Because the fee is agreed in advance, the issue of padding never arises.

The elephant in the dining room

The extent of "ordinary" bill padding may be the legal profession's proverbial "elephant in the dining room." Few in the profession want to acknowledge its presence, yet many — if pressed — admit that its effect is pervasive.

Perhaps it is the discomfort that many feel about looking too far into this particular Pandora's box that makes them express their concerns about the billable hour by focusing on the much more socially acceptable notion that, maybe, lawyers are being worked too hard because of high billable hour targets. That rather gentler expression of concern may be a surrogate for a thought that is far more disturbing — namely that the legal profession has overwhelmingly adopted a billing system in which dishonesty, in varying degrees, is not uncommon.

High billable hour targets may indeed encourage padding. However, if there is a problem, I suspect that it will never go away so long as the hourly billing business model remains dominant. Only by focusing attention away from time and onto value can the profession hope to rid itself of such a blight. And that, sadly, is unlikely to happen across the board.

15. The problems of excessive billing targets

To the extent that hourly billing presents arbitrary and unclear choices about how much, if any, time to record in various circumstances, lawyers are more likely to veer on the side of recording more when firms require attorneys to bill massive numbers of hours in order to remain employed. That raises the question about what number of billable hours is reasonable.

The production-line mentality

There is no doubt that the number of billable hours worked has risen over the past 20 years. This has come about as a natural consequence of the legal profession regarding "hours" as the basic measure of performance and productivity. Just as the owner of a factory wants its machines to produce more widgets, so the partners in a law firm want the lawyers on their payroll to bill more hours.

The point was made effectively by the late Chief Justice William Rehnquist, who observed in the mid-1980s that law firms bent on making as much money as possible treat associates "very much as a manufacturer would treat a purchase of one hundred tons of scrap metal."[7] He explained the prevailing attitude like this: "If you use anything less than the one hundred tons you paid for, you are simply not running an efficient business."

[7] William H. Rehnquist, *The Legal Profession Today*, 62 Ind. L.J. 151, 153 (1987).

The traditional 1,300-hour assumption

A study by the American Bar Association in 1958 — when the billable hour was advancing, but not yet triumphant — reportedly found that there were approximately 1,300 fee-earning hours in a year (this assumed that a lawyer worked half-day Saturdays).[8]

Let's assume that you work 48 weeks a year, allowing for vacations, national holidays, sickness, and so forth. The ABA's 1,300-hour number works out at just under five hours per day on the assumption of a 5.5-day week or around 5.4 hours if you amortize it over a five-day week.

The thought of anything close to a five-hour day may seem absurdly gentlemanly and leisurely to many who work in the legal profession. But the thinking behind the ABA's number was that there is, inevitably, a lot of *unbillable* time in a lawyer's day.

A commonly expressed view is that lawyers need to spend about three hours in the office for every two hours of billable time. The "unbillable hour" is taken up with all sorts of activities, such as dealing with administrative tasks, having lunch, shooting the breeze with colleagues, looking for things buried under piles of paper, recording time, dealing with personal matters — not to mention being distracted by bookmarks on the Internet. On that basis, the five-hour day requires a 7.5-hour commitment — which still sounds pretty civilized.

Anyone reading this book can tell that I do not favor aggressive billing. Nonetheless, I suspect that the ABA's 1,300 hour number is on the low side as a benchmark for the legal profession as a whole — and I'm not sure that a new ABA study on the subject would come up with the same number today.

That number can make sense for a solo practitioner — es-

[8] I have found numerous references to this study while researching this book, but its name and author(s) have proved elusive.

pecially since a solo lawyer will have to spend a fair amount of time running the practice as well as working on client matters. But it is unrealistically low for a full-time associate in a larger law firm whose involvement in practice management is going to be very limited. If ever the era of the 1,300-hour target did exist in law firms, it is not going to return. Maybe it should. But it won't.

How about 1,600-1,700 hours?

My view is that an annual target for an associate of around 1,600-1,700 hours is a reasonable compromise between the needs of law firms and individual lawyers to make money and the concern that excessive hours cause problems.

Here's how I get to that range. Again, I'll start with the assumption that a lawyer will work 48 weeks of the year. Let's assume that the lawyer is in the office — with enough work — on average from 8:30 AM until 6:00 PM. That's a total of 8.5 hours.

I recognize that some readers who rarely get out of the office before 9:00 PM will be rolling their eyes at this point. But I have never accepted that there is something about the practice of law that means that, come what may — even without the pressure of urgent deadlines — one has to work well into the night, every night, in order to do the job properly.

Good dentists don't go on drilling past the dinner hour when there aren't emergencies. Good attorneys need not go on lawyering that late either. Moreover, just as I wouldn't want my root canal done by a tired dentist, why should I — as a client — have my lease prepared by a worn-out lawyer?

It's one thing working late when the needs of the client demand it. And, often, a client's needs do. But the problem with the types of high billable hour targets that have become common in recent years is that they assume that lawyers will work long shifts *regardless* of the work they are doing. To stay on target, the lawyer has to work late even on matters that aren't especially pressing. The long hours are dictated not by the needs of the client, but by the revenue expectations of the law firm.

Anyway, back to my calculation of why 1,600-1,700 billable hours per year is reasonable, although not unchallenging. I suspect that most lawyers — assuming they have enough work and especially if they are not too heavily engaged in practice management — can do a bit better than billing two hours out of every three.

So I'm going to allow 6.5 hours as an average day's billing working those hours, which makes for 32.5 hours in a week. And I'll round that up to 35 hours, allowing for some longer days or work on weekends. Multiply that by 48 and you've got a total of 1,680 hours — call it 1,700 for good measure.

But I've worked out other scenarios where I end up with closer to 1,600 hours — and maybe less. For example, without that extra 2.5 hours per week that I threw into the calculation above, the total was 1,560.

The fact is that there is no objectively ideal number. However, I think that when one works the numbers of what is reasonable, civilized, and sustainable, while at the same time providing lawyers at all levels of the profession the opportunity to earn decent incomes, one tends to get something more or less in the 1,600-1,700 range. That is enough to be challenging, but not so high as to be soul-destroying or to virtually invite aggressive and suspect billing practices.

Heavy billers: 2,000+ billable hours a year

The reality, however, is that relatively few law firms set annual targets of 1,600 hours. A target of 1,700 is considered on the low side, and even 1,900 is middling. Those who aspire to be high fliers and earn the big bucks in private practice — especially in major markets — generally aim to work at firms where expectations of hours are in excess of 2,000 — 2,200, 2,400, and even beyond.

How is it even possible to bill that number of hours? One answer is that when dealing with all of the judgment calls about how to record time — the ones that have been discussed in this book — the lawyer has a huge personal incentive to come down on the side of charging the extra minutes.

This is how the two strands of the billable hours controversy intertwine. Some people focus on excessive hours as the essence of the problem; I, by contrast, believe that the billable-hour system is *intrinsically* flawed no matter how few or many hours are billed.

But, at the end, the two issues feed off one another: The system of counting hours leads to ever higher expectations about numbers of hours; and those expectations encourage lawyers to exploit the billable-hour system — with all of its anomalies and gray areas — in a way that makes it easiest for them to meet their elevated targets.

Life over 2,000 hours a year

But there is a limit to what can be done by aggressive billing alone. In order to be on the fast track in private practice in major markets, there is no doubt that a lawyer has to work very long hours indeed. And remember to get your flu shot — falling sick could play havoc with your career.

Let's consider what billing 2,200 hours actually involves. Doing the math, the lawyer who needs 2,200 billable hours over 48 weeks has to record an average of 45.8 hours per week, or about 9.2 hours per weekday. (Maybe you can get that down a bit if you make it up on weekends or skip vacations. But you get the picture. And, by the way, I'm assuming no padding.)

A "45-hour week" might not sound too bad. But remember that we're not talking about "a 45-hour week." We're talking about recording 45.8 hours of billable time.

In order to bill 9.2 hours a day, you'll very likely need to be on duty for a minimum of 12 hours a day — and probably longer.

Those types of hours aren't just when you're swamped — that's the *normal* work day. And if you don't have the work to fill those hours, you get panicked.

Add commute times and you're talking about selling your soul to the firm. If you have small children, you'll probably rarely put them to bed on weeknights — let alone have dinner with them.

But, even then, you might be panicking that you're not "performing" well enough. You know that some associates are billing 2,400 hours — and then there are the legendary stories of those who make it to 2,600. They are the true heroes, the ones certain to make partner.

Coyness about minimums

The firms that talk openly about their billing requirements tend to be those that boast how reasonable they are — the ones with targets set at around 1,600-1,700 hours.

Very few — if any — law firms publicly set minimum billing targets of over 2,000 hours. Often, in fact, big law firms state that they do not have "minimums."

However, the reality of working for them is that the expectations *are* there. The unofficial "minimum" turns out to be the number of hours you need to bill to get a bonus — and the real "targets" are the levels you need to reach in order to get the higher levels of bonus.

If you choose simply to opt out of the bonus rush, you'll very likely be opting out of the partner track — and, quite possibly, out of continued employment at the firm.

The money rush

The lawyer who bills 2,200 hours is going to be handsomely paid. Starting salaries for first-year lawyers at top law firms in 2007 were as high as $160,000 — and that's before bonuses. The bonuses typically kick in at around 2,000 hours, sometimes 1,900 — but the highest bonuses are for the higher numbers of hours.

Lawyers generally get yearly raises as they climb the seven-to-ten year path toward partnership — so a relatively new lawyer working for a top law firm can quickly make over $200,000 with salary and bonuses combined.

The new lawyers want the salaries. It's not just a matter of greed — it's also a matter of dealing with law school debt, not to mention enjoying a share of life's creature comforts.

The sharp rises in the expectations of what lawyers should earn that occurred in the past 20 years has been driven, in part, by the earnings of those who work in the financial services sector, which competes with the legal profession to recruit the brightest and the best. With investment bankers pulling in the truly big bucks, the legal profession had to offer better deals in order to tempt enough talent to want to make a career based on a bar card.

And the partners want the profits they will make off the new lawyers' time — a lawyer who bills 2,200 hours a year at, say, $350 per hour, stands to bring in $770,000 in revenue, less whatever gets written off. An army of bright, young things bringing in $350 an hour well into the night makes for very handsome incomes for their bosses.

Law firms indeed vie for top placements on profits-per-partner league tables, the most successful passing the $1 million-a-year mark.

Large law firms are structured like pyramids, with those at the top living off those underneath, the underlings performing sweat labor in the hope that they, too — one day — will climb toward the top and be allowed to profit from those below.

But the tickets up the pyramid are handed out only to those who earn their passage by stellar billing. Their motivation during the long nights of hard slog is that, some day, they will be invited to profit from the labor of tomorrow's pawns — those who, right now, are in law school, perhaps entertaining dreamy visions of law and social justice, but who, before long, will be drawn into the billing treadmill, tempted by the riches and egged on by the flattery of the recruitment process. Those newcomers will fill the places vacated by the lawyers who didn't make it or couldn't stand it, as well as by the much smaller number who did manage to make partner.

The system works on the assumption that most who are on the treadmill will never get to enjoy the riches. It's a matter of simple arithmetic: the higher the ratio of associates to partners, the larger the profit per partner is going to be. Law firms have an incentive to appoint only as many partners as they need to ensure that they recruit sufficient talent into the trenches and have a sufficient number of people vested in the firm so that it is properly managed, stable, and making rain.

Beyond that, it is better for the partnership if a lot of associates drop out and are replaced — especially as they reach the higher levels of associate salaries. So large law firms are happy to run a work regime that many will find unbearable. They want only the fittest to survive.

That said, life on top of the pyramid is not necessarily a bed of roses. The *California Bar Journal* reported in 2007 that even senior lawyers in big firms sometimes faced expectations of 2,200 hours a year — "or else."[9]

Are there such things as kinder-and-gentler law firms? Yes, but they tend to be smaller and mid-size ones.

The anxiety of life on the billing treadmill

Thus, from the beginning — and, perhaps, until the end — lawyers are under huge pressure to bill. This creates stress on a daily basis.

The new lawyer, in particular, operates under a mandate to record all time, but — often — with an instinct that much of that time really should not be billed. But one cannot afford to under-record time, because that would mean falling behind on targets — and once one makes a habit of that, it's very hard to catch up. And, perhaps, one comforts oneself with the thought that time recorded as "billable" is not necessarily "billed" — although usually it is, and one may never know either way.

The pressures and anxieties that all this creates were eloquently summed up in a blog entry by someone who now describes herself as a "recovering lawyer," but who previously operated in the world of "BigLaw" (a term often used to describe big law firms serving mostly big corporate interests):

"You fumble around on a project feeling like a

[9] *California Bar Journal*, "Growing, and Graying, Attorney Population Hits Retirement Age," July 2007.

> complete idiot, with time ticking away, and at the end of two and a half hours you've been down half a dozen blind alleys and have half a paragraph of tepid conclusions and realize you don't really understand what you're supposed to be doing anyway. Do you bill that 2.5 hours? On the one hand, great, 2.5 hours, that's a nice big chunk of billable time — great! I hope this will take me a lot longer to finish up. On the other hand, you realize, someone's going to look at this piece of paper and think, "We've hired us a complete idiot! It took her 2.5 hours to do this simple project, and she's still not finished." Maybe you should only write down 1 hour. But where are you going to get the other 1.5 hours? Stay later? What if while you're trying to catch up you're only slightly less clueless? You can see how anxiety-producing it all is."[10]

The anxiety often doesn't go away. And so long as you have to meet a stiff hours requirement, any day on which you fall behind creates a need to make up. And if you slip much behind the curve, it's hard to get back on top. It's stressful.

There's "good stress" and there's "bad stress" in the practice of law. "Good stress" comes from the demanding nature of the work. If you aren't feeling that sort of stress, it may mean that you aren't challenging yourself. "Bad stress," by contrast, has to do with reaching your hours target and the various political issues that go with it. That one can do without.

---

[10] Extracted from a posting titled "Billable Hours" made in 2004 in a now-inactive blog called "Stay of Execution" written by someone with a pen name of Scheherazade. Reproduced under that blog's Creative Commons License.

Part Three: Rebellion & Inertia

16. The backlash

The backlash against the billable hour began not all that long after it established its hegemony. As noted in Chapter 2 dealing with the history of the billable hour, the American Bar Association published a critical study as long ago as 1989.

However, it was the rapid rise in billable-hour targets in the nineties that began to increase the intensity of the criticism.

The 2002 ABA report

Another ABA report, published in 2002, concluded that what it termed "the overreliance on billable hours by the legal profession" had resulted in a wide variety of negative consequences for both lawyers and clients.[11] The ones that it identified included:

- Billing that does not reflect value to the client.
- Discouraging attorney-client communication.
- Penalizing the efficient and productive lawyer.
- Failing to discourage excessive layering and duplication of effort.
- Not rewarding the lawyer for productive use of technology.
- Creating conflict between clients' and lawyers' interests.
- A decline of the collegiality of law firm culture.
- Discouraging lawyers from taking on pro bono work.
- The client running the risk of paying for the lawyer's incompetency or inefficiency.
- The padding of time records.

[11] ABA Commission on Billable Hours Report, 2001-2202.

That should have been something of a wake-up — the American Bar Association, no less, talking about the prevalent system of billing in the United States bilking clients through padded time records and subsidizing inefficient lawyers in relationships where attorneys and clients have conflicting interests.

The then-President of the ABA, Robert E. Hirshon, wrote in a preface: "It has become increasingly clear that many of the legal profession's contemporary woes intersect at the billable hour."

Five years later — in 2007, weeks before this book was published — the *ABA Journal* ran a cover story whose title was: "The Billable Hour Must Die." Written by lawyer and novelist Scott Turow, its subtitle (at least on the online version) was: "It rewards inefficiency. It makes clients suspicious. And it may be unethical." The article concluded (referring to the legal profession): "Somehow, people as smart and dedicated as we are can do better."

The backlash from the bench

Judges, including those at the highest levels, also began to speak out. In 2001, Supreme Court Justice Stephen Breyer, addressing the American Bar Association, said:

> "How can a lawyer undertake pro bono work, engage in law reform efforts, even attend bar association meetings, if that lawyer must produce 2,100 or more billable hours each year, say sixty-five or seventy hours in the office each week? That kind of number reflects a pace, which, according to one lawyer, is like "drinking water from a fire hose." The treadmill's pressure is partly financial, aggra-

> vated for younger lawyers by law school loans that may amount to $100,000 or more, which must be paid back from their earnings in practice."[12]

Justice Breyer returned to this subject on a number of occasions, including in a commencement address in 2003, in which he surveyed the manner in which the billable hour was reshaping the practice of law. He concluded:

> "These problems may seem minor compared to problems such as racial or gender inequality or global warming, problems that American lawyers have helped, or are helping, to overcome. But they threaten our profession."[13]

These sentiments have been echoed by many other judges in both trial and appellate courts. This includes remarks made in published opinions dealing with attorney fee issues. Take, for example, the following criticism by a federal district court judge:

> "The problems created by billable hours have brought about a storm of criticism directed to the legal profession, especially when there are excessive billable hours.... [A]n attorney billing an excessively high number of hours needs counseling, not praise. A true professional goes considerably be-

---

[12] Remarks by Justice Breyer in opening keynote address, "Our Civic Commitment," at the Annual Meeting of the American Bar Association. Chicago, IL, August 4, 2001.

[13] Remarks by Justice Breyer, Boston College Law School commencement, Newton, MA, May 23, 2003.

> yond practicing law "by the numbers." The time and time sheets should, at best, be only a rough guide or starting point and not the master of relations with clients (or those ultimately responsible for the payment of the bill)."[14]

Using even stronger language, an opinion by the Florida Court of Appeals referred to "the notorious 'billable hours' syndrome, with its multiple evils of exaggeration, duplication, and invention."[15]

In a lighter vein, the California Court of Appeal noted in an unpublished decision:

> "Whether the emphasis on time spent has... actually served the "prestige" of the legal profession is — as [in] the joke of the 40 year-old dead lawyer who arrives at St. Peter's gates and is assumed to have been 120 when he died based on his billable hours — open to question."[16]

Mitigation at the margin

Despite the intensity of criticism, not much has occurred to change the system of billable hours. It is true that many law firms have tinkered with it at the edges. It is quite common, for example, for firms to offer arrangements to mothers with young children that involve a reduction in hours (and salary) without automatically stepping off the partner track. However, these

---

[14] *Avila v. Coca-Cola Co.*, 728 F.Supp. 685, 715 (M.D.Fla.,1989).

[15] *Miller v. First American Bank and Trust*, 607 So.2d 483, 485 (1992).

[16] *Ernsting v. Pacific Bell* (2000 WL 34532109).

don't exactly result in soft workloads. Typically, one would be talking about something like a 20 percent reduction.

Likewise, larger firms have become more organized in encouraging and allowing pro bono work. Many, indeed, use the lure of pro bono opportunities as a bait to tempt new hires coming out of law school who still cling to lofty, public-interest ideals. The most progressive large firms, such as Morrison & Foerster, have full-time pro bono coordinators.

However, some of the efforts to deal with the harsh effects of billable hours are intended not to reduce workloads, but, rather, to make super-high workloads more sustainable. These include the taxi rides home late at night, the sushi deliveries so that lawyers can have dinner at their desks, and — in some firms — the "concierge" services that take care of personal chores.

In short, it would be unfair to say that *nothing* has changed as a result of the backlash against the billable hour. However, change has only come at the margin. And it is patchy. For all of the criticism directed against it, the billable hour still reigns supreme.

17. Why good lawyers don't change a bad system

Why has the billable hour, a product of the second half of the twentieth century, become so entrenched and powerful that few predict its demise despite the barrage of criticism it faces?

Whatever the reason, it isn't because it enjoys a huge amount of positive enthusiasm. Rather, the reasons involve a mixture of inertia, lack of interest, convenience, and perceived self-interest.

The Excel-ization of the practice of law

One of the reasons for the billable hour's strength has to do with the trend for law firms to become larger and run more like corporations. From the bean-counter's point of view, hourly billing makes a lot of sense. If you know how many lawyers you have, you can easily set up budgets and forecasts. You can track who is most productive and whose productivity is trailing.

By analogy, if you're running a hotel operation, you know how many rooms you have and you strive to get as close as possible to 100 percent occupancy at rack rate. You can track your progress on spreadsheets.

So, too, with law firms. If you have 200 lawyers, billing an average of $300 per hour, your annual revenue goal is to get as close as possible to 200 x $300 x (say) 2,000 = $120,000,000.

Realistically, you won't hit that goal — there will be laggards within the ranks and write-offs. But you can benchmark your performance, and work on dealing with the parts of the practice that are a drag on the rest. You can play around with your numbers, doing "what ifs?" with regard to headcounts, hourly rates, and billable-hour targets. It is the "Excel-ization" of the practice of law.

The "don't change the system *now*" factor

But there are more fundamental reasons, as well. One has to do with the attitudes of those who have ascended into the ranks of partnerships having sweated for years as associates billing huge numbers of hours in the hope that, one day, they, too, would enjoy the spoils. They haven't toiled all those years just so that they — on reaching the top — can change the system into something kinder and gentler.

Fear of reduced earnings

This last point is part of a bigger issue, which is that there is a widely held view — not wholly unjustified — that lawyers earn more if they stick to hourly billing and that most of the alternative, so-called "value-driven" systems are a fancy way of cutting bills and, hence, hitting incomes. Looked at that way, it's a tough sell to get law firms to abandon the billable hour in droves.

I don't think that alternative billing *necessarily* leads to lower incomes even in the short run. Consider, for example, the earlier discussion in this book about the "under-appreciated brilliant hour." But the fact is that it often does.

If all the problems with the billable hour didn't hit the client in the pocket, it wouldn't be worth all the fuss — at least, from the clients' perspectives. Unless one were obsessive about the intellectual basis for how a bill was arrived at, one wouldn't really care. Individual lawyers might not love the billable hour because of the "hour" factor. But for clients, it's the "bill" that counts.

So perhaps the most fundamental barrier to encouraging lawyers to think again about the billable hour is the fact that — at least in the short term — you appear to be asking them to make less money. Somehow, that doesn't sound like a compelling rallying call.

That said, even if lawyers look at this issue purely from a self-interested way, they shouldn't assume that sticking with the billable hour is necessarily the smart business decision.

Self-interest involves looking beyond immediate income. It involves considering how alternative forms of billing might help grow a practice by attracting and retaining clients who, otherwise, might go elsewhere. It also involves thinking about how it helps attract and retain good lawyers.

In a competitive market, law firms can grow by differentiating themselves. Adopting different billing methods offers a more convincing means of doing so than the vague, self-indulgent fluff typically found on law firm Web sites.

The fact is that in other fields of human endeavor, simply extracting as much money as possible out of each customer in the short term may not be the best formula for growth in the long term. Look at Southwest Airlines and compare it with former rivals whose names one no longer even remembers.

And if revenues do fall on given matters, so, too, can costs. Again, consider Southwest. The law firm that thinks differently when it comes to billing methods also has an opportunity to develop alternative approaches to overhead.

That is a subject for another day and another book. For now, suffice it to say that despite the technological revolution of recent years, there has been remarkably little change in how law firms are generally organized. The time may be ripe for the reinvention of the law firm in ways other than billing.

Furthermore, if alternative billing does mean that more people have access to less expensive legal services, that might not be a bad thing. The cost of legal services has become so high in recent years that increasingly few people can afford them. At some level, that cannot be good for the profession in which all lawyers, collectively, have an interest.

Lack of interest and risk aversion

Another reason why the billable hour seems so resilient to any amount of criticism is that many lawyers have surprisingly little interest in the whole subject of how law firms should be operated as revenue-earning enterprises. Lawyers tend to harbor some general notion that they should make as much money as possible, but, beyond that, many aren't really all that interested in the business model.

Moreover, of those lawyers who do have some interest in the "business side" of running a law practice, many don't have much of a clue when it comes to things like marketing and brand development. They might be perfectly fine lawyers. They may even be excellent business lawyers. But they may not be particularly inspired businesspeople themselves. Maybe that's why they became lawyers. And this means that they don't readily engage with questions about how things could be done differently from what they have grown used to throughout their careers.

Likewise, lawyers tend to be risk-averse. Their work might be stressful for all sorts of reasons, but — usually — not on account of personal risk. Billing by the hour suits that temperament. Stepping off the straight-and-narrow path and thinking and acting differently does not.

Even solo practitioners — who have done something entrepreneurial by setting up on their own (sometimes by choice, sometimes by necessity) — tend to want to emulate bigger firms. Consider, for example, the awkward efforts that many go to in order to make it appear to clients that they are a "firm" rather than a one-person shop.

There is, in short, a remarkably passive attitude within large parts of the profession — an uncritical and almost uninterested acceptance of a way of doing things that has been handed down on a plate. That, coupled with the "if it ain't broke" — at least from the revenue point of view — "don't fix it" attitude, means that a lot of lawyers really aren't all that engaged with the subject of how to bill.

They'd rather be billing than analyzing the billable hour. And when they're done billing, the last thing they want to think about is the billable hour.

Those are the lawyers who, perhaps most of all, need this book. Unfortunately, they are the ones who are least likely to be reading it.

Acquiescent clients

If enough clients rebelled against the billable hour, it would, no doubt, eventually collapse under market pressures. Part of the reason why it is so enduring is that although a lot of clients grumble about their bills, and mutter criticism about billable hours in general, few demand something different (other than in those areas of the law — such as personal injury and criminal defense — where other forms of billing are common).

Corporate, in-house lawyers who hire and deal with outside counsel typically themselves once worked for law firms where they billed by the hour. They might be aware of the system's flaws, but they also have a certain comfort level with it. No one ever got fired for signing a fee agreement with outside counsel based on hourly billing. Hourly rates also make it superficially easy to comparison shop. And they fit well into the spreadsheets and management reports prepared by in-house-counsel who need to report to their superiors how much lawyering they are actually buying each month.

As for noncorporate clients, they, typically, don't have enough confidence or understanding to challenge what appears to be the norm. For example, the one-time participant in the litigation market is unlikely, at the outset, to take on the status quo. Even if that private litigant ends up somewhat the wiser, he or she probably has neither the motivation nor the muscle to change things for others.

The challenge of implementing change

Another reason why hourly billing is particularly entrenched at the corporate level is that although there are alternatives, they can be challenging to implement. In particular, it's all very well talking about "value-based" billing, but how can one assign "value" to the myriad of services that a law firm might provide to a corporate client?

Would it just be a matter of replacing one form of arbitrary billing system with another? Would the law firm and corporate client have to negotiate endless mini agreements, or would the client just leave it up to the judgment of the lawyers to "do the right thing" when it comes to preparing bills? Neither option seems very satisfactory.

I'll return these concerns shortly when the focus of this book shifts to examining the alternatives.

18. The rules about fees

The debate about billing at times seems deadlocked between those who seek change and those who have little interest in the subject so that they simply rest on the status quo and don't even engage. Some support for reformers can be found in the rules of professional conduct under which lawyers ply their trade.

A reference point: ABA Model Rule 1.5

The American Bar Association's Model Rules of Professional Conduct, which have been adopted by some states and are influential in others, provide a good reference point for what is a "national" standard. (To the extent that anything is "national" in the American legal profession.)

And, as shown below, the ABA rules appear to suggest that a blind, slavish adherence to the billable hour — such that *nothing* other than time spent is even considered — may not satisfy a lawyer's ethical obligations regarding the setting of fees.

Specifically, the ABA Model Rule regarding fees says this:

> *Rule 1.5: Fees*
>
> (a) A lawyer shall not make an agreement for, charge, or collect an unreasonable fee or an unreasonable amount for expenses. The factors to be considered in determining the reasonableness of a fee include the following:
>
> (1) the time and labor required, the novelty and difficulty of the questions involved, and the skill requisite to perform the legal service properly;

> (2) the likelihood, if apparent to the client, that the acceptance of the particular employment will preclude other employment by the lawyer;
> (3) the fee customarily charged in the locality for similar legal services;
> (4) the amount involved and the results obtained;
> (5) the time limitations imposed by the client or by the circumstances;
> (6) the nature and length of the professional relationship with the client;
> (7) the experience, reputation, and ability of the lawyer or lawyers performing the services; and
> (8) whether the fee is fixed or contingent.

That sounds mighty like a formula encouraging value billing. Going down this list, it is clear that the time a service takes to provide — although a legitimate factor in assessing reasonableness — is only one of many factors.

Is it ethical to ignore value?

The wording of ABA Model Rule 1.5 tells us that the factors it lists are "*to be* considered" (not that they "may" be considered) — suggesting that consideration of all of them is mandatory for those lawyers operating under those rules. To that extent, it is questionable whether an automatic "don't even think about anything else" policy of charging by the hour does satisfy the ethical requirements of the ABA Model Rules. Although lawyers might settle on a pure hourly rate, they are required to, at least, *consider* other factors besides time.

Those other factors include "the novelty and difficulty of the questions involved, and the skill requisite to perform the legal service properly" (factor 1 on the ABA list) and "the amount involved and the results obtained" (factor 4) — considerations that are at the core of value analysis.

The "results obtained" factor appears to contemplate that the reasonableness of a fee has to be revisited at the end of a representation in the light of what was accomplished. I don't believe that the value of a lawyer's services necessarily diminishes if the outcome is not successful. Lawyers who take tough cases aren't going to win all of them — and losing doesn't mean that they didn't deliver full value in their efforts.

That said, results can impact reasonableness. For example, a fee that might be unreasonable under some circumstances may seem more reasonable in the light of a good result.

Of course, all lawyers are governed by the rules in their own jurisdictions. Most rules do list various "fee factors" very similar to those in the ABA rule, but some have a different preamble.

For example, in California — where I practice — the rules don't require a fee to be "reasonable," but simply say that it should not be "unconscionable." (See California Rule of Professional Conduct 4-200.) That seems to give a lawyer more leeway in fee setting — I'm not sure that a fee that is not "reasonable" is, per se, "unconscionable." And if I'm right about that, it means that a California lawyer *is* allowed to charge an unreasonable fee — so long as it isn't *too* shocking.

Still, the California rules do require the lawyer to go through a checklist that is the same as that in ABA Model Rule 1.5 in order to determine whether a fee *is* "unconscionable." In essence, this amounts to applying "value-oriented" considerations in establishing whether a fee does conform to the required standard.

Part Four: Better Billing

19. A dozen better ways to bill by the hour

The focus of this book is about to switch to the alternatives to the billable hour. But before going there, and recognizing the reality that most law firms are not going to abandon the billable hour, here are 12 ways in which the concept can be made more benign:

1. Talk to your client for free: Consider a radical step — *don't bill your time for talking with your client.* This might be more practical in some matters than others. There are instances where communications with the client form a very high proportion of total time and, where that is so, writing off all your client communication time would mean working for little pay.

But in a lot of other cases, client communications are a relatively small proportion of the total. In those cases, adopting a "no-charge" policy can alleviate some of the concerns about hourly billing without costing the lawyer too much. Most obviously, it addresses the issue about the chilling effect that the ticking meter can have on attorney-client communications.

The anomalies about six-minute minimums and increments don't go away if you stop billing for client communications, but they may, at least, become less glaring — charges that reflect these types of anomalies tend to be especially grating where the client was a part of the billed-for communications. There must surely be nothing worse than a call from a client saying: "I *know* that call didn't last six minutes." And even if a client doesn't actually call and tell the lawyer that, there's a good chance that the thought is there anyway.

Even if the nature of the representation means that not charging for any client communications isn't practical, consider not charging for very short or incidental ones. Limit the charges to those communications where you were substantively counseling the client as a lawyer.

2. Don't charge for perfunctory communications in general: Consider not charging for other phone calls that last only a few minutes. Likewise, don't charge for most short emails.

Some lawyers argue that they have to record even very short events, because the purpose of time records is not just to generate bills, but also to keep a log of activity that may be needed for other purposes — for example, establishing the fact that certain communications took place and defending against malpractice claims. Fair enough. But the fact that something goes in a time record does not mean that it *has* to go on the bill.

3. Ban the 12-minute minimum and increment: When you do bill for short events, apply six-minute minimums — not 12-minute ones. And if you are charging for very short events, batch them together rather than applying six-minute minimums to each. Even if you do apply 12-minute minimums, don't go up in 12-minute increments after that — stick to increments of 0.1 hours.

4. Charge less for mundane activity: Charge half your normal hourly rate for travel and waiting time.

5. Be careful about multiple meters: Don't make a rule of charging for more than one lawyer's time when two lawyers talk about a case unless both are adding value. For example, the delegation of a task from one lawyer to another is really an internal management function for which a client shouldn't have to pay. Arguably, neither lawyer's time should be charged when that takes place.

6. Keep targets reasonable: Avoid annual billable hour targets of more than 1,600-1,700 hours. If someone has a crazy year and goes overboard with their hours, that's fine — and doubtless they should be compensated for their extraordinary efforts. But this shouldn't translate into a policy that requires or even encourages mega-hours.

7. Allow pro bono to count toward targets: Allow reasonable amounts of pro bono time to count toward a firm's billable hours requirement. It's good for the practice of law. And it's good for a law practice — savvy lawyers know how pro bono work can — despite its altruistic nature — help the development of paying business.

8. Train lawyers about time: Give new lawyers in your firm training about how time should be recorded. Don't just tell the new lawyer: "Record all your time." Address the practicalities and detail of what this involves. Produce a written set of policies. Have them read this book!

9. Produce detailed descriptions: Provide reasonably detailed logs that describe the work performed during time that is being billed. The whole point of hourly billing is meant to be its "transparency." So, for example, don't merely log a phone call as having taken place. Indicate what it was about. Don't just log: "Review documents, 3.2 hours." Indicate what documents and why. That makes you more accountable for the value delivered, even if you are charging for time.

10. Think value: Likewise, even though you are billing by the hour, analyze the value given before you send out the bill — write off time when there is a clear disconnect between the time and the value. Don't charge for learning on the job when the client had a reasonable expectation that the lawyer(s) it was hiring knew how to do the task already. By all means show the time you have written off as a "discount" if you want to earn kudos.

11. Consider hybrids: Even if you aren't willing or able to cast aside the billable hour in its entirety, consider hybrid arrangements that allow individual fee agreements to contain some aspects of alternative billing. The next few chapters should give you some ideas.

12. The smell test: Apply a simple test in deciding what to do and what not to do: "If the client knew what I was doing and my mindset in doing it, would I be embarrassed?" If the answer is "yes," don't do it.

A 13th suggestion: Don't nickel and dime with expenses

Actually, I'll throw in one other suggestion and make this a baker's dozen. This one isn't strictly about fees, but it is closely related. It has to do with the other thing that goes on the bills you send out — expenses.

Few things are more off-putting to clients than the sense that they are being nickel-and-dimed. Therefore, think very hard about what types of expenses you are going to try to recover.

Maybe there was once an era when long-distance phone calls were so expensive that they were a legitimate cost to pass on. (Remember the old movies, where people would drop everything because someone was "calling long distance?") But those days are past. You are charging enough for your time in talking on the phone. Trying to recover the cost of the call is petty.

The same goes for ordinary first-class postage. By all means charge for the cost of sending out a Fedex, but don't charge for first-class mail. (I remember once hearing a story about a law firm that sent out a bill whose only item was the postage cost of the previous invoice it had sent out. Can that be true? Who knows?)

Some firms levy some sort of a percentage surcharge to cover miscellaneous overhead expenses — for example, a 2.5 percent amount added to every bill. This reminds me of irritating cover charges. Or arbitrary "resort fees" in hotels. Charges like this annoy clients. What would you think if your car mechanic added a percentage to the bottom of the bill to contribute toward overhead? Your clients probably think the same if you do it.

Charging for online legal research services like Westlaw and Lexis is another practice that annoys people. In the past, these services operated on a "transaction" basis — law firms paid by the search or retrieved document. These days, however, virtually every law firm has a flat fee allowing unlimited use of the portions of the service to which it subscribes. (If there are still firms out there that aren't on a flat fee, they're nuts.)

Despite this, some firms continue to charge clients per Westlaw or Lexis transaction — often profiting on the subscription. Others divide up the flat fee so that clients pay an amount corresponding to their percentage use of the service that month. (That is an odd arrangement, because the amount a client pays becomes a function not just of how much the service was used on that client's behalf, but how much use of the service was made on behalf of *other* clients.)

Neither method of passing on the cost makes any sense. Clients aren't charged a "book fee" if a lawyer goes into a firm's law library to conduct research. The lawyer's time in doing so is already being compensated. Therefore, it is irrational to charge for use of similar materials just because they happen to be online.

What's more — despite a common misconception — the online legal research services really are not that expensive compared to the legacy, hard-copy alternatives. In fact, in my practice, I would pay much more if I maintained an old-fashioned law library than the amount I pay each month to Westlaw.

Legal research is central to the practice of law. Charging extra for the tools is like a hotel charging extra for use of beds.

I could give other examples about nickel-and-diming, but the message can be summed up as follows: *Keep your bills clean and simple.* Do not add lists of "extras." Ultimately, they do you more harm than good.

The only expenses you should seek to recover are those that involve payments to a third party of an identifiable and non-petty amount that you have incurred specifically in connection with your work on a particular matter and that would not have been expended otherwise. Even then, don't mark up the costs.

You'll be surprised at how much goodwill this type of policy engenders. And guess which bills clients pay the fastest — those that irritate them or those that they think are fair?

It's not simply about short-term revenue

A common reaction to the suggestions in this chapter — and to much of what is written in this book — will, no doubt, be that it is simply a manifesto for lawyers slashing their bills and, hence, their incomes. And who in the legal profession wants to line up behind that ridiculous idea?

But it isn't as simple as that. See my comments in Chapter 17 about how, putting aside short-term revenue effects, alternative billing can help to grow a practice. Actually in this chapter, I haven't even gone very far up the "alternative" route. For that, you need to read on.

20. Alternative billing overview

Now to the tough part. It's one thing pointing out the flaws with the billable hour. It's another coming up with alternatives.

That said, there *are* alternatives, which are already in daily use by lawyers who, for whatever reason, are not wedded to selling their services in six-minute parcels. I know — I am one of them. If you move beyond the billable hour, you may be departing from the norm — but you will not be heading up a path on which no other lawyer has yet to tread.

Before getting into the alternatives, let me just say that it may not be until you move away from the billable hour that you realize just what a millstone it has been in your professional life. There is a sense of liberation. Of spring in the air. Trust me, it is worth it. And if, by chance, you don't like it, you can always go back. Although I suspect that few do.

As a roadmap for the discussion that will follow, here are four broad categories of alternative:

1. Result-oriented fees: This is where all or part of the fee depends on the outcome of a case. This includes the classic contingent fee — widespread in personal injury — which is the best established and most common of all of the alternative billing methods. However, result-oriented fees can have wider application (especially when combined with other fee arrangements).

2. Flat fees: This is where a lawyer quotes a fixed price for a matter at the outset. The price quoted is the price paid, so long as the work stays within the agreed scope. A variation —

which makes sense when it seems too difficult to know in advance what work will need to be performed — is to have a series or menu of fixed fees for different possible components of an overall course of representation.

3. Budget-based billing: This is where a lawyer handles a matter on a not-to-exceed budget. Up to the budget, the lawyer may be charging by the hour or by some other method. But there is an agreed cap beyond which the fee will not go.

4. Value-based fees: This is where a flat fee is not agreed at the outset, but the lawyer instead charges an amount based on an assessment of the value delivered, taking into account a variety of factors — including the time that was spent. This, in essence, is the "old-fashioned" method of billing — discussed in Chapter 2 dealing with history — that predated the onslaught of the billable hour. However, in its reinvented form, the client can be involved in the process of determining the amount that should be paid.

Hybrids

This list is by no means exhaustive. In particular, one can devise hybrids — for example, a flat fee with a success-based bonus.

Hybrids need not only blend different forms of alternative billing. One can also have a hybrid that blends the billable hour with an alternative method. For example, a reduced-rate hourly amount with a success-based bonus. Of course, hybrids that keep the timekeeper's meter ticking are always still subject to many of the underlying concerns about hourly billing in general. But they can be a whole lot better than the billable hour in its unadulterated form.

One type does not fit all

Keep in mind that a billing method that might work in one context may not be applicable in another. For example, a risk/reward-sharing system such as contingent fee billing really doesn't work with most transactional types of law, such as preparing a will or drafting a contract. This is because there is no clearly quantifiable "reward" or "risk" to share.

This is in contrast to hourly billing, which — if one can live with all of its flaws — does "work" in just about any context. In other words, if you want a universal method of billing, you are probably stuck with the billable hour. But why fixate on having a one-size-fits-all solution?

With those thoughts in mind, let's take a closer look at each of the alternatives.

21. Result-oriented fees

With billable hours, the lawyer expects to be paid regardless of the outcome. And the more expensive the legal services are to the client, the more profitable they are to the lawyer. The interests of lawyer and client are thus in tension.

One form of alternative billing is to try to give the lawyer and client a common set of interests. This involves giving the lawyer a material stake in an outcome.

The purest form of result-based arrangement means that the lawyer is paid solely as a percentage of a client's monetary recovery. However, there are also other forms of result-based fee arrangements, such as outcome-related bonuses.

Contingent fees

The contingent fee — also known as "contingency" fee — is the "no-win/no-fee" type of arrangement that you see splashed across billboards and Yellow Pages ads. It is so common and well-entrenched in parts of the legal market that, arguably, it doesn't really count as "alternative." But it is an "alternative" in the sense that it doesn't utilize the billable hour.

In its classic form, a lawyer takes no fee whatsoever unless the client obtains a monetary recovery. If there is a recovery, the lawyer takes a percentage.

Probably the main reason why contingent fee billing has remained strong over the years is that it principally targets the sector of the market that usually can't afford to pay by the hour. Indeed, as the cost of civil litigation has risen, the contingent fee's advantages have become even more obvious.

The contingent fee is most common in personal injury, wrongful death, and employment cases — the areas where people on "ordinary" incomes are most likely to be involved in litigation and where, typically, there is insurance money on the defense end, meaning that a judgment is likely to be paid. That said, it sometimes also features in commercial litigation.

The origins of the contingent fee

The contingent fee is much older than the billable hour. It goes back to the nineteenth century. And although different legal historians have reached different conclusions about when it began, there is evidence that its use extends back to the early part of that century.[17] By contrast — and as noted earlier in this book — the billable hour came into being in the second half of the twentieth century.

As one scholar has argued, the contingent fee's deep historical roots cast doubt on three criticisms directed against it: (1) That it is a product of the late nineteenth century development of the modern tort system (and hence a fit target for tort reform); (2) that it is a partisan mechanism designed for a society riven by labor strife (and thus unnecessary in a more peaceful and prosperous era); and (3) that it is simply part of modern-day ambulance chasing.[18]

Rather, the deep roots of the contingent fee highlight its association with the strongly felt American desire to ensure access to courts for both rich and poor alike. This approach was reflected in the Sixth Amendment's guarantee of the right to counsel, in the various due process provisions of the Fifth Amend-

---

[17] *The History of Contingency and the Contingency of History*, Stephen Landsman, DePaul Law Review, Vol. 47, No. 2, 1998.

[18] *Id.*

ment, and in the rejection of the British rule requiring the loser to pay the winner's attorney fees in most civil litigation.

However, the contingent fee is a much more recent development elsewhere. In Britain — where it is known as the "conditional fee" — it did not become permissible until 2000. Traditionally, "no-win/no-fee" schemes were regarded as "unprofessional" in Britain and prone to encourage litigation. Eventually, those views became discredited. What is surprising is how long that took to happen.

While discouraging "unnecessary" litigation may be a legitimate public policy, it seems absurd to forbid a type of fee arrangement on the grounds that allowing it would result in more lawsuits. If one doesn't like lawsuits, the underlying laws should be changed. It makes no sense to outlaw particular types of fee arrangement to discourage citizens from asserting rights under laws that do exist.

Contingent fees and case screening

For obvious reasons, contingent fees are associated with the plaintiff side of lawsuits — it is the plaintiff that stands to make the monetary recovery, a percentage of which can be shared with the lawyer.

Contingent fees are, indeed, sometimes associated in the public perception with trigger-happy lawyering by the plaintiffs' bar. They tend to get mixed up with the so-called "frivolous lawsuit" (to use a term much favored by certain politicians as well as business and insurance interests eager to promote tort reform).

In fact, that association is unfair. The lawyer who takes a case on a contingent fee has a much stronger personal interest in ensuring that it is viable than one who is going to be paid by the hour no matter what the result. And the most accomplished contingent fee lawyers are very selective about the cases they take and skilled in the art of screening them.

Why contingent fee windfalls are necessary

Contingent fee billing meets a great need. Without it, many people with legitimate grievances would never get their day in court. But it comes at a price. In order for lawyers to offer contingent fees, there has to be a prospect of a sufficiently large recovery that compensates for the risk that they might not get so much as a bean for their services.

To put it another way, a successful contingent fee lawyer has to make windfall amounts on some cases — more than would be earned by the hour — in order to cover others where there is no recovery.

Inevitably, this can breed resentment when a lawyer makes, say, 40 percent on a $500,000 settlement relatively early in a case. That gives the impression of being exorbitant. And, looked at in isolation, it is.

But the client is, effectively, subsidizing other cases that the lawyer took on and lost. Without this subsidy, the lawyer wouldn't have been in a position to take on the case that *did* lead to the recovery. At least, that's the theory.

The subsidy also extends to cases that go to trial and are won, but where the time investment is grossly out of line with the contingent fee received. Many cases on a contingent fee do not "pencil out" if taken to trial, even if there is some recovery.

Because contingent fees can lead to windfall amounts for the lawyer, those who are in a position to pay their lawyer — rather than having the lawyer assume the risk of the case in return for a cut of the action — may be better off ponying up the money. That said, there is something inherently appealing about the "no-win/no-fee" approach that makes it attractive even to those clients who are in a position to pay and even when it may not be wholly rational. Perhaps it is, in part, to do with getting away from the billable hour.

Problems with contingent fees in smaller cases

Unless the potential amount of damages is sufficiently large, it may be uneconomical for a lawyer to litigate a case on a contingent fee. For example, if the largest possible recovery is, realistically, only $20,000, a contingent fee is not going to yield more than around $8,000 at best — and there is only so much lawyering that can be expected for that amount, whatever the billing method.

Some lawyers do take on contingent fee cases where the damages potential is relatively low. However, they tend to have an incentive to settle them early — even if this means a substantial reduction on what the case might theoretically be worth if litigated somewhat longer.

For example, if a lawyer can earn 40 percent of $10,000 by settling a case very early on, it can be a lot more efficient than going potentially the whole way in the lawsuit in the hope of getting 40 percent of $20,000.

In some ways, this gives the attorney a conflict of interest with the client. The attorney has an incentive in obtaining a fee in the most efficient way (which isn't necessarily a matter of going for the largest fee by doing a lot more work); the client, by contrast, really just wants the largest recovery.

That said, if it wasn't for the contingent fee system, the client might not have an attorney at all. And settlement early in a case eliminates the risk that, by litigating longer and harder, the client might lose — meaning that there would be zero recovery.

Mitigating the effects of contingent fees

There are ways of mitigating the effects of the contingent fee. One is to have a scale of percentages depending on the time at which a case settles or is decided. For example, an early settlement could result in a smaller percentage than a win in front of a jury. However, if too much of the "windfall" factor is removed, the lawyer may feel that there is an insufficient upside to rationally justify the downside.

Outcome-related bonuses

Although the purest form of contingent fee is the no-win/no-fee version in cases where the goal is to obtain a money judgment, one can devise any number of variations and hybrids. These include fee agreements where there is some underlying guaranteed fee — which could be a flat fee or (if you must) an hourly one — that is topped up with a bonus depending on the outcome.

These types of arrangements are still "contingent fees" in a literal sense, in as much as the amount that is paid is contingent on what happens. However, the term "contingent fee" tends, in practice, not to be used to describe bonus arrangements and generally refers to the "no-win/no-fee" variety.

Some clients like outcome-conditional bonuses, because there is an added incentive compared with a fee system in which the lawyer doesn't share in any of the fruits of a successful outcome.

There might be something in that. Personally, however, I find that I work in the same way regardless of incentives. I'm happy to accept a bonus for a successful outcome. But I don't find that the presence of such a bonus arrangement in any way affects the quantity or quality of work I do on a case.

Where a lawyer should be careful is in accepting bonus

arrangements under which the fee-plus-bonus total is simply equivalent to a normal rate for the job. If that is what it amounts to, the lawyer isn't so much earning a "bonus" for a successful outcome as suffering a "penalty" for an unsuccessful one. There's nothing inherently wrong with that, but just be aware of what you are agreeing to.

Outcome-related fees linked to nonmonetary outcomes

One can also have contingent fees and other outcome-based arrangements that relate to some result other than a monetary recovery — the enforcement of a contract or property right, for example. Here, the fee would need to be fixed in advance, because it couldn't be expressed as a percentage of anything.

That said, contingent fees linked to nonmonetary outcomes can be tricky, because it isn't always easy to define whether a particular goal *has* been achieved. Whereas with monetary outcomes, the result is pretty clear-cut, nonmonetary results can be a bit fuzzy.

For example, one could have a situation where a goal was *virtually* achieved, but not quite — even though what was accomplished wasn't at all bad. It would be unfair for the lawyer to miss out on a fee. Other forms of alternative billing may make more sense in such a circumstance.

Defense-oriented contingent fees?

Contingent fees are generally associated with the plaintiff side of lawsuits. However, one can devise defense versions as well. That is especially so if the goals are nonmonetary — for example, "I will pay you a fee of $30,000 if you ensure that my neighbor does not get an easement across my land."

In theory, one could also have a defense contingent fee

linked to a monetary outcome. For example, a lawyer defending a case could — if successful — be paid a percentage of whatever was considered the "exposure" in the lawsuit. Thus, if the exposure were $1 million, the lawyer would be entitled to, say, 30 percent of that amount in the event that the plaintiff recovers nothing. For every dollar in damages paid to the plaintiff, one dollar would come off the fee.

The obvious flaw in that example is the difficulty of establishing the "exposure" amount on which the percentage would be based. Also, the risk is that a lawyer would lose any incentive to perform if — during the course of the litigation — it became clear that there would be a recovery that would wipe out the fee, even though there was still much to fight for in terms of how large the damages would actually be. Maybe this could be addressed if the arrangement were set up so that for each dollar of damages, something less than a dollar came off the lawyer's fee — so that the lawyer and client were, in effect, splitting the damage.

So that type of contingent fee is not without problems, although there may be ways of working around them. But I offer it as an example of how there is scope for creativity in fee setting. Rather than always working off fee-agreement templates, lawyers and clients should spend more time working out customized arrangements for specific cases. In some instances, a one-of-a-kind agreement can be the best type.

22. Flat fees

Next, to my own favorite type of fee arrangement — the flat fee. With this method of billing, the lawyer and client agree on a fee at the outset. Regardless of the time spent or the outcome, that is the fee that is paid for the scope of work that it covers. That scope of work may be the whole course of a matter, or it may be one component part.

Settling into the flat-fee mindset

The instant reaction to flat fees among many lawyers is something like: "Yikes. If I set the fee too low, I'll end up working for nothing."

Setting a flat fee at the right level is, indeed, tricky — but the lawyer will *never* end up working for "nothing." Rather, the lawyer will always work for the flat fee that was agreed (assuming that the fee is paid — and I'll come to that later).

"Working for nothing" anxiety only applies if the lawyer continues to think in terms of billable hours, even when not actually charging that way. Lawyers with that anxiety are mentally dividing the flat fee by an hourly rate and fearing that after a certain amount of time has been spent, everything else will be unpaid labor.

But with flat fees, one has to stop the clock as much as possible (keeping in mind that there may be circumstances when you do still need to keep some record of time spent — more on that later, too). The idea is to liberate the lawyer from the tyranny of six-minute increments. Enjoy the freedom. Don't treat flat fees as an overlay to a rotten system. It is a *replacement*.

Clearly, the amount of time that will likely be spent will be a major factor in setting a flat fee. However, a variety of other factors should also enter into the analysis. These include:

- The difficulty and novelty of the work.
- The results that you feel you may be able to obtain, and what this is worth to the client.
- How interested you are in doing the work.
- The extent to which taking the case will preclude you from doing other work.

In other words, it's not unlike the multi-prong analysis in the American Bar Association's Model Rule 1.5 — discussed in Chapter 18 — that addresses whether a fee is "reasonable."

The critical importance of defining the scope

An absolutely critical prerequisite to working with flat fees is that a lawyer be very precise in defining the scope of what's covered.

An open-ended flat fee that covers any possible development can be a black hole that results in a lawyer feeling underpaid for the sheer amount of work undertaken when the matter involves unexpected tasks. And a dispute with a client about whether something *is* covered suggests that not enough time was spent at the outset thinking about, and defining in writing, what actually *was* to have been covered.

My own law practice is focused exclusively on appellate work. The course of an appeal is more predictable than litigation in a trial court, but appeals can still take unexpected twists and turns. Thus, in my fee agreements, I am *very* specific about what is and is not covered and about the point at which covered services terminate.

Defining the scope of work means putting a lot more thought into drafting fee agreements than many lawyers are used to. Whereas hourly fee agreements are often templates with little customization, my flat-rate ones are heavily tailored to the circumstances of each specific case.

Although preparing this type of fee agreement consumes a lot more time at the front end than heading up the hourly path, that is counter-balanced by the fact that — going forward — you won't have to spend time recording your hours. And do not underestimate how time-consuming it is to record your time — at least, if you want to do it well.

Of course, you can — under some circumstances — have an all-embracing, no-exclusions flat fee. But that is likely to be priced higher than one with limitations concerning the scope.

As for work that may prove necessary and that isn't covered by the scope of a flat fee, one option is something in the initial fee agreement to the effect that — if and when this occurs — you and the client will confer about an appropriate fee that will reflect the value of the additional services provided, as well as their complexity and the time involved.

If that sounds too uncertain, you can provide for hourly billing as the fallback unless the client and you agree to something else. The utility of the billable hour is as a universally applicable fallback solution in the absence of any other arrangement. And occasional resort to billing by the hour may provide a reminder of how good it is to have gotten away from it for the bulk of what you do.

The difficulty of setting fees in civil lawsuits

The major difficulty with flat fees occurs when one doesn't really know in advance what services *will* be required. In that circumstance, it can be a tall order to set a flat fee that seems fair to both sides for an entire course of representation.

With civil litigation in trial courts, it is especially hard to quote a flat fee for an entire case at the outset. You don't have control over the course and scope of what will ensue. For example, your opponent might drown you in work involving motions and discovery. You can do your best to make predictions, but it can be pretty hit or miss.

And although the vast majority of civil lawsuits do not make it all the way through to trial, some do. Thus, it would be reckless to base fees on the assumption that a case will settle or be dismissed, but probably mighty expensive for the client to work on the assumption that it will go all the way.

The flat-fee solution for civil lawsuits

So other than in relatively straightforward matters, I'm not sure that setting flat fees to cover *entire* civil lawsuits is practical.

However, don't assume from this that you're condemned to a life of billable hours as a civil litigator. There is a way to make flat fees work in this type of situation.

Rather than attempting to assign a flat fee to an entire lawsuit, one can apply fixed prices to its component parts as one goes along. This can be done in one of two ways: You can either quote a flat fee for a "phase" of a lawsuit — defined either temporally or by procedural status — or you can have a series of fixed fees for individual tasks within the lawsuit.

For example, you can charge a flat fee for drafting a complaint or, perhaps, to get a lawsuit through the pleadings stage. Motions of various types can be billed on a flat-rate basis. Routine court appearances for status conferences or hearings on motions certainly can be.

In some cases, these fixed fees for specific tasks can come off a menu of set charges, rather than being assessed on a case-by-case basis. Something as straightforward as a routine court appearance need not be quoted individually any more than a routine procedure by a dentist such as filling a cavity. Rather, one can have a "list price."

In other cases, a custom fee probably does need to be assessed taking into account the circumstances and complexity of the case. For example, you could quote a fee for handling all of the depositions that your client will take in a lawsuit or for all of the written discovery it will be propounding. Likewise, although it would probably be somewhat arbitrary to set a list price in your practice for "any" type of motion for summary judgment, once you are familiar with a case, you could set a flat fee for such a motion in that particular matter.

Under this type of task-based billing system, a fixed fee can also be applied to cover routine communications and other odds-and-ends work that might be too small to quote separately. Consider it as an overall "case handling charge," if you will. To the extent that some significant work might be performed for which no fixed fee has been assigned, one can always agree that hourly billing will be applied as a fallback.

Flat fees outside civil trial courts

Compared with litigation in trial courts, arbitration can lend itself more easily to flat fees that cover an entire case, since the scope of discovery and motion work is generally considerably less. Hence, the scope of what will need to be done is more predictable.

Flat fees are also more practical — and very common — in criminal defense work. There, the scope of work is more predictable than in civil litigation. Again, the big difference is that discovery — that black hole in the world of civil litigation — is far more limited.

Likewise, with many business and real estate transactions, the course and scope of legal work is sufficiently predictable to make flat-fee billing viable. The same applies to services involving probate and estate planning.

By "predictable," I'm not talking simply about the amount of time that will be spent, but also about the nature of the work that will be performed and the value of what will be delivered. As suggested earlier, setting flat fees should not be viewed simply as a matter of estimating hours.

Another type of engagement that works well for flat fees is one which, at least initially, involves giving the client an opinion, as opposed to embarking on a course of conduct. Here, the attorney is analyzing a set of facts that could lead to a lawsuit or a transaction — or to neither — and the client wants advice on what to do.

For the most part, this type of service can be provided for a flat fee. Even if the subsequent course of representation would be difficult to quote on a flat-fee basis, the initial advice should lend itself to that type of arrangement.

Retainers for areas of ongoing advice

Another version of the flat fee is where a client pays a lawyer a monthly fixed retainer — or, maybe, a quarterly one — intended to cover routine consultations on matters that are expected to arise.

For example, an employer might have an arrangement with employment counsel that covered ongoing advice on the myriad of issues that routinely crop up in the workplace. If any issue blew up into something bigger, it would then be charged for separately. But the retainer would cover general counseling. Periodically, the size of the retainer could be reassessed in the light of the quantity and complexity of advicc bcing provided.

Flat fees and refundability

Clients generally like flat fees. But sometimes, they will result in a lawyer receiving *more* than would have been paid under an hourly arrangement. This can occur if less work proves necessary than was envisaged at the outset.

That said, flat fees that are completely nonrefundable can run into ethical problems. In 2009, for example, California was considering introducing a provision in its Rules of Professional Conduct making it unethical for a lawyer to charge a nonrefundable fee (except for a "true" retainer whose purpose is *solely* to reserve the lawyer's availability). I suspect that some other jurisdictions have similar provisions.

This type of rule appears mainly targeted at iniquitous arrangements where a client changes his or her mind about wanting to proceed with a matter and cannot obtain a refund of a fee advance paid. In that scenario, the lawyer is being paid for work not performed. But this rule also implicates flat fees in situations where services *are* performed, but a matter comes to a conclusion somewhat sooner than had been envisaged. There can be something of a gray area between a situation where a service was fully performed but involved less work or fewer steps than had been expected to reach a conclusion, and another where a representation was terminated prematurely meaning that the service was never fully performed.

Even before this rule change, my fee agreements provided for partial refunds if a case settled or otherwise terminated before a certain stage in the process. Among other things, that answers one of the criticisms of the flat fee, which is that it discourages settlement because the client may have no fee-based incentive to terminate the litigation early.

Flat fees and the lazy lawyer

A possible concern about flat fees is that a lawyer can have an incentive to do as little work as possible. Just as hourly billing rewards inefficiency and gives a lawyer an incentive to perform unnecessary work, so flat rates might tempt a lawyer to do only the minimum.

This is, potentially, a real problem. Advocates of flat-rate billing should not dismiss it. The best response is that clients who have that concern about a particular lawyer are probably looking at the wrong lawyer. A good lawyer will want to do the best job possible on every case — not just as a matter of professional ethics, but also because one's reputation is ultimately of far greater importance than the money one makes on any given matter. In my practice, for example, there is no better method of getting new business than being able to list wins in matters already concluded or providing references from satisfied clients.

To put it another way, there are good lawyers and bad lawyers out there, whatever type of fee arrangement is in place. In selecting a lawyer, a client shouldn't promote the type of fee arrangement ahead of the quality of the lawyering. That was a point I made in the introduction to this book.

Flat fees and the creative lawyer

With the right lawyer, by contrast, flat fees can result in useful work that might not have been done with hourly billing. This is because they enable the lawyer to develop legal theories in a creative way, without constantly worrying whether exploring certain avenues can be justified by the extra hourly charges. The lawyer billing by the hour might skip certain things that might prove worthwhile, reckoning that the client wouldn't want to be billed extra or can't be counted on to pay.

The challenge of setting flat fees

In order to quote a flat fee as a lawyer, you need to have a keen appreciation of the market in which you operate. Position it too high and you'll drive business away. Position it too low and you may also drive business away — on the basis that you might look too "cheap" to be good.

Unlike the hourly billing lawyer who just makes one pricing decision — setting a rate — the lawyer who bills on flat rates makes numerous pricing decisions. Unless one's practice involves a succession of tasks for different clients that are more or less the same, each matter has to be priced separately. For example, in my practice, I can't just quote a single price for bringing or defending an appeal. I might be able to quote general ranges, but I need to look at each case individually before coming up with a specific price.

The ongoing need to come up with fee proposals is one reason why flat rate billing can be hard to implement in larger firms, even when minds are open to moving away from the billable hour. Whereas hourly billing provides a law firm's management with easy control over pricing, flat rates can present a difficulty — they either require pricing decisions to be delegated to individual lawyers or workgroups or they require lawyers to get approvals from management each time they take on a new matter.

That said, the delegation of pricing decisions to the lawyers who will perform the work can have beneficial consequences. Potentially, it empowers workgroups and encourages them to be more entrepreneurial and client-focused in their pursuit of business.

Flat fees in other professional environments

Moreover, flat fees are used in comparable professional environments. For example, McKinsey & Company — a leading business consulting firm — generally charges flat fees. Its professional consultants don't even have hourly rates (although they do have per-diem rates for internal job costing purposes).

There are, of course, conceptual differences between the type of work a firm like McKinsey does — which involves assigning teams to study complex but probably defined issues — and some of those that law firms do, which can often involve undefined or bits-and-pieces assignments. Nonetheless, the McKinsey example shows that flat-rate billing is not inherently impossible in a large professional-services firm. Moreover, the fact that McKinsey — a firm at the very top of the management consulting field — has adopted flat-rate billing for its *own* business model says something about the inherent benefits of that system.

Why flat-fee lawyers may still need to record time

In some circumstances, lawyers who charge flat rates may still want to — and, maybe, need to — record their time.

One reason is that it can help you to determine what fees to quote in the future if you know how much time you actually ended up spending on similar matters in the past. Even though the zen of flat rates means that you shouldn't simply estimate what an hourly fee would have been, time is clearly one of a number of important factors.

Another reason to track time may be that you hope that the other side in litigation will end up paying your client's attorney fees. Although the general rule in the United States is that each sides pays its own fees in litigation regardless of the outcome, parties often enter into contracts that contain a "loser-pays-fees" clause. Moreover, there are some statutes that provide for the loser to pay fees in particular types of lawsuits.

There is no intrinsic reason why fees in these circumstances need be calculated by multiplying hours spent by an hourly rate. The entitlement provided in contracts and statutes is generally to "reasonable" attorney fees — and, as the American Bar Association's Model Rules indicate — a "reasonableness" analysis implicates a variety of factors besides time. However, as a practical matter, courts generally look to time spent as a starting point in their decision about how much fees to award.

Quite often, courts do mark down the requested fees if they feel that the hours are excessive for the work that needed to be done. Judges are often the biggest skeptics when it comes to billable hours and may adopt something resembling a value analysis when determining what is "reasonable." However, they still generally want to know about time spent — and, the more detailed the information, the greater the chance the lawyer has of recovering the full amount requested.

Thus, a lawyer would risk compromising a claim to fees by walking into court saying: "Your honor, I have a flat-fee agreement with my client. I really don't know how many hours I spent. But this is the flat fee that my client incurred."

That said, the lawyer might get the requested amount by saying: "Your honor, I'm not sure exactly how many hours I spent, but I am certain that it was more than the number you get dividing my flat fee by a reasonable hourly rate." Still, this might invite a response from the other side: "How *can* you be certain of that if you didn't track your time?"

So the fact is that it is much safer to track your time if part of the end-game in litigation is getting the other side to pay your fees. I wish that weren't so, but it is.

Clients who take unfair advantage

One of the benefits of flat fees is that they encourage attorney-client communications. That is a good thing — up to a point. But the point is crossed if a client takes unfair advantage of a flat fee and expects to spend an inordinate amount of time engaging a lawyer in circular conversations going over ground that has been amply discussed already.

This type of client may have some type of emotional or psychological need to speak constantly with a lawyer, such that the conversations cease being about anything that is within the boundaries of a regular attorney-client relationship. And it can get quite ugly if one tries to truncate the communications.

Still, this is not an inherent drawback of flat-fee billing. This type of client would most likely prove to be a nightmare whichever billing method you employed. For example, you might find it difficult to get paid for the endless phone calls if you were charging on an hourly basis.

The fact is that just as there are lawyers whom wise clients should avoid hiring, so there are clients whom wise lawyers should avoid representing. The alarm bells should sound in the initial screening process.

That said, if your client screening system does let you down — as eventually it might — there are protective measures you can have in place. This involves careful drafting of fee agreements. In particular, I would advise including in the scope of work a "reasonable" amount of client communications. Do not commit yourself to talking with a client on an open-ended basis. You do not want to become a flat-rate amateur shrink.

Flat fees and the art of collection

Lawyers who charge by the hour may well often end up billing more than those who charge flat fees. However, billing is not the same as *collecting*. A benefit of flat fees is that they substantially increase your chance of collecting every penny on the dollar.

There is far less scope for arguments about the bill. Moreover, when you quote flat fees, it's much more practical to ask for the entire fee to be paid in advance.

With my standard fee agreement for new clients, I do ask for the entire fee to be paid upfront. This is then deposited in my client trust account. I don't draw a penny until I file a brief on the client's behalf. This arrangement provides comfort to both sides: I don't get paid until I have performed; but I know that I'll be paid when I do perform.

This type of arrangement may not work for everyone — in my case, it typically means that I don't draw any revenue until I have worked on a case for about six months, often longer. But I find it fosters a general sense of mutual trust in the attorney-client relationship.

By contrast, it's much harder to ask for the full fee to be paid in advance if you bill by the hour — not least because you don't know what the full fee is going to be. And as the billable hours mount up (and especially if progress proves disappointing), collection can become increasingly problematic.

Do flat fees scare clients away?

One of the arguments I have heard against flat fees is that they scare clients away by putting too much focus on the "big number" at the outset. A flat fee of, say, $25,000 can sound more daunting than a request for a $3,000 advance against billable hours costing $350 a shot — even though the billable hours may well end up adding up to a whole lot more over time.

In other words, it may be easier to sign up a client by not focusing on the entire fee. Even if asked, one can fudge or offer the vaguest of nonbinding estimates. Once the client realizes how many hours are being racked up — some way into the representation — it may be impractical to change course. The client will, effectively, be locked in (so the theory goes).

If that strategy does hold, it is simply another example of how the billable-hour culture involves glossing over detail and keeping clients in the dark. But I am skeptical that the billable hour is a good bait with which to lure clients. Too many clients have been burnt too badly in the past. More and more are looking for something different.

In my experience, clients are willing to contemplate — and, indeed, advance — the "big number" if it's fair and if they can lock in. And a client who is scared away by a flat fee may well be the type who would be a problem-payer when it comes to hourly bills anyway.

23. Budget-based billing

One of the things that clients dislike about hourly billing is its seemingly open-ended nature — the fact that the bills know no limits and that the more costly the representation becomes, the more profitable it is for the lawyers.

The benefits of budgeted maximums

Flat fees are one way of addressing this concern. However, an alternative for those lawyers unwilling to head up that path is to bill by the hour but to cap the amounts with budgeted maximums.

The benefit of this type of arrangement is, potentially, that the lawyer operates utilizing what may be a preferred method — time-based billing — but the client knows in advance what the worst-case fee could be.

Indeed, some clients might prefer hourly billing with budgeted caps to a flat-rate system. This is because with flat rates, there is always the possibility of the fee turning out to be rather high if, for whatever reason, the matter ends up coming to a conclusion with much less work than anyone had envisaged.

The drawbacks of budgeted maximums

However, budget-based billing can also end up offering the worst of all worlds. Until the cap is reached, there are all the drawbacks of the billable hour — with its anomalies, arbitrariness, structural inaccuracies, and so forth.

Then, once the cap is passed, the lawyers think they are working for free — and that's not something that is going to inspire or motivate them to do their best work. That's because, unlike their flat-rate counterparts, they haven't really shed the time-based billing model in favor of a value-driven alternative. They are still thinking in terms of selling time as their commodity.

Budget-based billing also runs into the same problems as flat-rate billing, but without yielding all of the latter's advantages. In particular, there is the challenge of determining in advance what the scope of the work is going to be in order to come up with a cap that makes sense.

So this isn't a method I would generally encourage. But it has its adherents.

Budget-based hybrids

As with other methods, one can devise hybrids that make budget-capped billing more appealing. For example, one can have a cap, but with a success-related bonus if there's a good outcome. As always, it makes sense to think creatively about billing options, rather than to assume that a few preset templates are all that's available.

24. Reinventing value-based billing

The last of the alternatives is something of a throwback to the past — but with a twist designed to make it more acceptable in the present.

Value-based billing the old-fashioned way

If you read Chapter 2 outlining the history of the billable hour, you'll know that before lawyers started working out their bills by multiplying time spent by an hourly rate, they sent out monthly bills that they felt were "reasonable" for work done taking into account a host of factors, of which time was one.

The methods by which the amounts were arrived at were not exactly transparent. Indeed, the amounts charged could seem somewhat arbitrary. But, with a fair and ethical lawyer, trusted by the client, this could be a flexible formula for arriving at a value-based amount.

The problem, though, is the built-in conflict of interest. Lawyers have an interest in charging as much as they can get. Clients are wary about amounts that have neither been agreed to in advance nor are based on objective factors.

A modern twist: client-empowered "value adjustment"

A Seattle law firm with about 25 attorneys called Summit Law Group operates what appears, in essence, to be a modern incarnation of the pure value-driven model.

Its approach to making this work — given the mistrust that can arise when the lawyer alone is left to come up with a figure — is to empower the client with what it calls a "value adjustment line" on its bills. As it explains on its Web site: "We empower each of our customers with the right to adjust our billing, upward or downward, based on our customer's perception of the value received, not ours."[19] It describes this as the "cornerstone" of its billing approach.

The Summit Law Group doesn't appear to use a single form of billing that gives rise to the number that is subject to "value adjustment" by the client. It sometimes bills by the hour, but generally favors a more value-driven arrangement even before adjustments are made. It says that it is "open to any creative billing arrangement that is fair." These include:

- Value-based billings with incentives for results that exceed expectations.
- Monthly retainers for day-to-day advice.
- Percentage fees, success-based fees, and other fee incentives.

If slavish adherence to hourly billing seems wrong, if contingent fees aren't appropriate, if flat rates seem problematic, and if budgeted caps don't appeal, then why not just fall back on value? That really should not be a shocking suggestion. Something is amiss with the profession if it sounds quirky to suggest that lawyers' bills should reflect the value of their work.

---

[19] www.summitlaw.com. It's worth taking a look at this firm's Web site to get an idea of how a mid-size law firm can implement alternative billing and — judging by its client list — succeed. Also, the firm seems to take a fresh approach to other areas of law practice management besides billing. Incidentally, I have no connection with that law firm and, prior to writing this book, had never communicated with anyone connected with it.

Wrapping Up

Conclusion

No system of charging for legal services is perfect. And if one spends too much time focusing on the subject, one risks "paralysis through analysis" — the state in which every option, including the status quo, seems so flawed that one finds it very hard either to make a change or to positively commit to not changing.

But if this book has achieved anything, it has been to draw attention to the fundamental flaws of the billable hour. The case to try other options is compelling. The alternatives are not without problems, but they are better.

There is good reason to believe that alternative billing is making advances. However, there is little prospect that the "alternatives" will become the norm. Being an alternative biller is a little like being a Mac user in a Windows world — one smugly uses a system that is widely regarded as superior, but that nonetheless has a single-digit market share. Go figure.

Indeed, what is frustrating about the billable hour is its seeming invulnerability despite the singular lack of enthusiasm among those who labor daily under its burden.

So here is a challenge: If the billable hour is to reign supreme, it should at least have a good advocate. Someone should write *Hurray for Billable Hours* — a book designed to extoll its virtues and answer its critics. There is no such book at present. Let there be a better debate.

But I suspect that no one will write such a book. Because there really wouldn't be much to say.

Prove me wrong if you disagree.

About the author

John Derrick is a California attorney with a solo practice focused exclusively on appeals and related matters. He is certified by the State Bar of California Board of Legal Specialization as a Specialist in Appellate Law.

He received his undergraduate degree in Britain at the University of Oxford and his law degree at the University of California at Berkeley, Boalt Hall School of Law.

Before entering the legal profession, he co-founded, operated, and eventually sold two niche information publishing businesses in the UK and US. He also served as Special Adviser to the Energy Secretary in the British cabinet.

He lives in Santa Barbara, California, with his wife and two children. He is an eager traveler, who has visited 82 countries and is aiming for 100.

He uses flat fees in his practice whenever possible. You can find out more about him from his law practice Web site at www.californiaappeals.com.

A review of this book

"*Boo to Billable Hours* is a "must read" for any attorney who ever has prepared a time sheet. Any client who ever has paid a time-based bill should read it, too.

"In this lively, engaging, and pithy book, John Derrick explains why hourly billing often encourages inefficiency and sometimes facilitates fraud. Mr. Derrick discusses a wide array of issues and problems involving the hourly fee, including record-keeping, double billing, the use of minimum billing increments, billing targets, and the quandary of how to bill for travel time. He offers sensible and practical guidance for time-keepers on these and other issues, and he also explores the advantages of alternative forms of billing, including result-oriented fees and flat fees.

"Avoiding any hint of "lawyer-bashing," this book evinces a profound respect for the legal profession and seeks in a constructive manner to help lawyers formulate fees in a manner that is consistent with high ethical standards and the needs of clients."

Review by William G. Ross

- Professor of Law, Cumberland School of Law, Samford University.
- Author of: *The Honest Hour: The Ethics of Time-Based Billing by Attorneys* (Carolina Academic Press, 1996); *Legal Fees: Law and Management* (with John W. Toothman, Carolina Academic Press, 2003); and various articles concerning the ethics of hourly billing.